Into The Soul Of A Woman

A Poetic Journey From Tragedy To Triumph

Tamika Wells

Into the Soul of a Woman
A Poetic Journey From Tragedy To Triumph

Published by :
Tamika Wells Consulting
www.TamikaWells.com

Initial Edit by Lori Jensen
Second Edi by Claudia Cramer, CSC Professional Editing Services
Front Cover Design by Amanda Fernandez
Back Cover Design by Claudia Cramer, CSC Professional Editing Services

Into The Soul Of A Woman

A Poetic Journey From Tragedy To Triumph

By Tamika Wells

*He restores my **soul**…*
Psalms 23:3a

Published by
Tamika Wells Consulting
www.TamikaWells.com

Dedication

Dear Mom, though we've had our ups and downs, you've introduced me to an unshakeable faith that carries me through. You did your best in spite of adversity and I thank you. I look forward to seeing you and all my loved ones again. In this life, I'll still continue to represent you well and make you *all* proud!

This book is also dedicated to every woman who feels like she has a hole in her soul but finds healing in just being herself.

Special thanks to all who dare to read this book! And all who are trying to understand the mystery of a woman's soul. WE LOVE YOU AND THANK YOU for your continuous love, allyship and support!

Table of Contents

PREFACE

Be prepared. This book is designed to reveal, to redeem. Meaning, you may need a box of tissues, a friend to call, a counseling appointment to sort through the emotions, the triggers these poems will raise. The good news is, with the right self-care plan in place, you're going to be just fine!

Hello, I'm Tamika Wells, your soul physician for today! No, you don't have to call me Dr. Wells. I'm not much into formalities. No, let's sit in a circle as a group. Or let's sit knee to knee across from each other, one on one. I want to look you in the eyes, dear sister. We've been through a lot, haven't we? No worries though! We've also had a lot of smiles, too! If not, hopefully you will by the end of this book.

Do you like yourself?
Can you say you completely and deeply lovvvve yourself?
Not sure anymore?

It's OK!

Let's begin the journey to friendship with ourselves through poetry. So glad to have you along with me!

From My Soul to Yours

I'm handing you a magic wand. You get to keep it! Wave it and make a magic bubble appear around you. Take it on this journey with you as you read this book. It will keep people from hearing you cry. It will keep people from judging your face. It will keep others from hearing you scream or shout as loud as you want to. This magic bubble is your safe place. Permission to sit in your emotions, GRANTED! Sit next to them in the backseat of your life. Look them in the face, because right now, you don't have to drive. What are your emotions saying? What do they look like? Ask them what gift do they have for you today? What are they trying to say? They have a place. It's your turn and your time!

(Most emotions only last about five minutes, so no Sis, you won't fall apart.) Just lean in!

Love & Relationships

Even as children,
women are groomed
to build their identity around
who they love
and who loves them.
How do you see yourself
when you have it all
or neither of them?
How do we deprogram,
address messed up itsh
and find contentment?

Break & Just Let It

It's ok to break.
It's ok to regret
The choices we make.
Cry it out
Until you surrender.
And remember,
We're only human,
Looking for love
From broken humans.

It's just a matter of
Finding someone
Willing to work on their
Pieces. Their peace
While you work on yours.
Not someone so caught up
In the outward
That the inside is rotten,
Long forgotten

But heaping a stench
The closer you get.

It's about being ok
To learn from mistakes.
And find out what you do
And don't want.
Not letting your past
Haunt you
To the point you're afraid
To try again and again.
Be your best friend, first!
"Girl, don't put up with that!"
"Dude, I see the red flags,
You don't have to take that!"
Your self-talk
Is the most important talk;
Give yourself some credit!
Speak good things to yourself
And expect it!
And when you find true love
Over time...
Just let it.

Who Are We Fighting?

Who are we fighting?
Going all in like
One is the monster under the bed,
The very thing that
Dominated us
As a helpless child,
And we swore NEVER again.
What you're saying about me,
Did I really do?
The negativity I feel about you,
Is it true?
Or are we shadow boxing
Our past?
The traumas of yesterday?

Do you see it?
I'm not Momma

Daddy
Brother
Sister
Ex-lovers;
I'm me.
But the hurt and pain
Won't let you see
Nor hear me.

I'm trying to see
You,
Not them.
All the men
That abused or neglected;
Their sin is not yours.
My tears aren't all you,
Just the soreness
In my soul,
Haunting me
Foreboding joy...
As you hold my hand,
Will this happen again
Or are you a different man?

As I struggle to love you
For you
And not what and not who
I've dealt with before,
I feel our dreams
Crashing to the floor.
Though we thought
We could be so much more,
But we're fighting the wrong things
In the wrong way
With the wrong people;
Even fighting wars within,
Labeling it sin
When it is pain
Which is so human.
But will we give
Each other permission
Grace...
To be human
And listen?

Let's undo shame.

Guilt is tearing us apart.
Isn't it nailed to the Cross?
Because my past pain
Isn't your mistake.
Because your past pain
Isn't my mistake.

It's a choice we
Can't escape
When two broken people
Want to make
A whole life.
And new love cuts like a knife.
Steps on glass shards
From the past,
Broken apart.
Jagged pieces
Of healing hearts,
Touching together
And it hurts so good.
But it hurts so bad.

From fixing to fighting

And you take personally
My sad,
But it's not yours
And it's not mine.
Let's walk to the trash can.
Empty it out,
Counsel it out,
Peroxide it out,
And move on.
So that the new pain
Won't fester upon
Old wounds.
There will be new
Pain.
It's a part of life
But it'll cause less strife
To clean out the old,
Assign it a new home
Away from our
Newfound peace
In you and me
In Christ.

All of You, So Beautiful

(In Response to a "Christian" Narcissist)

Maybe...
But it's the way you see
On Earth, Jesus wasn't a dictator,
Not authoritarian, but authoritative leader.
He asked questions.
"Do you want to be made whole?"
Understanding and honoring
The will and choices of the human soul.
He gave it to us.
He made us.
He meets people where they are.
The Kingdom that He brought to Earth
Didn't make women walk beneath
His feet in the dust.

He even took good care
And honored Mary while
He was dying on the tree.
The first person to see Him
Live again, at the tomb
Was a woman, Magdalene.
He shared special revelations with her.
What you believe doesn't even line up
With your ministry or Scripture.
I heard your leader's heart firsthand
By the Word of God,
Man & Woman stand together.
They communicate;
They collaborate;
They talk and plan together.
Iron sharpens iron.
Two are better than one.
A child left to his own demise
Becomes a shameful son.

So, I ask you...
Where does this need to
Control one,

To suppress others to feel good
Come from?
It's not who you said you were
In the beginning
Before we started sinning.
Dominion is not for the person
Who doesn't see all parties winning,
And in Christ's light shining.
We are a city
On a hill,
Light not meant to be
Under a bushel.
Thankfully, in January 2021,
He gave me direct instructions.
You call ego but
It's a reflection
Of the you that you don't like.
Her driving abilities
That Christ uses effectively,
Respectfully,
Without controlling,
Because she yields it
All to Him.

He doesn't push her to sin.
But He loves
Her drive,
Her smile,
Her collective wins
For all, not just self.
And she's beautiful,
And tasteful,
And willing to listen;
Scrub floors
While driving a Benz;
Wise, loveable and
Peaceable.
Embrace her in you
And there will be
Peace, blessings and
Honor in Christ's kingdom
That you steward.
Less toiling by the sweat
Of your brow,
Less attitude,
Less lust for power,
As you unify the inside

And your mind
With the Word,
The mind of Christ,
And His will
And all of you
So beautiful
Will shine through.

No Traction

No traction.
I give you no action.
I spend no passion
On narcissists.
Wanting to get a rise,
Even to make me cry.
For what?
When my gut told me
You were no good.
But like a chameleon,
You morphed into
The perfect companion
So quickly.
Up close and personal,
Beyond my boundaries.
Hearing, but not hearing me,
I end at your means.
I said I wanted to live righteously.
I said I'm afraid to fall.
You said, *God understands.*

I'm here though;
Your brothers and fathers
From church aren't.
I helped you with your son.
I helped you with your business.
I helped you feel protected.
What I do makes sense.
I saw you
When they made you feel invisible,
Used and misunderstood.
So why would you resist me
When I see your heart?
Let's be indivisible.

Because your heart is dark,
You want to do things to me
In secret.
Your love is fleeting
And not what I've asked God for.
Though I'm in this wilderness,
No one else around,
I won't let you trick me
Into jumping down

Or groveling at your feet.

No traction.
No action.
I'm not making my own bread
Or bed.
I'm Spirit-led
And there's something twisted
About what you said
About your use of His Word.
You're saying one thing
While I'm watching your outward.
It doesn't match up.

And now I go silent.
Not responding to your texts
Or screenshots.
Manipulations
To make me afraid to lose love
Or triggered
And offended to argue or fight.
I put you before the Lord
In prayer;

At the same time,
Healing
To get far out of your reach.
Even the devil can preach,
Angel clothed in light.
So your words are like
Sweet, savory arsenic biscuits
With honey butter.
Or spicy hot wings,
Sent to get a reaction.
So no traction
Cuz I'm covered
In His anointing oil,
Holy Spirit viscosity.
Silently slipping
From your control
Like a football
Covered in oil.
You might have won me before
But not today
I won't be foiled.

Eve slipped up

When she gave you her ear.
Jesus overcame you for me,
So, get behind me, too!
Even if man isn't there
In this wilderness,
I'll depend on God's principles
To carry me through
Without you
Tempting me to give up power
And offering me things
That don't belong to you
But are already mine.
You're evicted
And restricted
From residency in my heart
And mind.
You'll waste no more of my time.
No traction.
No action.
Blocked, deleted and out of sight.

Jealous

I'm jealous of the sun
On your cocoa magic skin.
I'm jealous of the dirt
That gets felt and squeezed
By your strong finger tips.
I'm jealous of their smiles
When my sexy man
Walks by.
Can I be the sweat
Kissing your brow?
Or at least wipe it away?
Am I a damsel in distress
Fainting on the couch of love,
Helpless every time you go away?
Begging you,
How long will you be gone?
When will you be here to stay?
And do you really feel the same?

I don't think you know
What I go through
When there's tragedy
And I can't hold you...
So forgive me
If I cling
To the hope of
You tinkering with *my* things
And all the joy you bring,
Forever holding you near.
But hope now is better,
Much better than fear.
Forgive me but
It's hard to go
A day without you,
Never mind 20 more years.
I'm jealous...

You Ready?

I thought I was ready
'Til I had to write that check.
You thought you were ready
Until I needed you to listen
Instead of playing Mr. Fix it.
We've all gotta a lotta
Growing to do.
But it behooves you
To think you're ready
If you can't receive this truth.

Thank you for the basics.
Work on that common decency.
Thank you for showing interest
But I'm old enough to know
This is not what I need.
For me, life is too short
To take a risk
For you to figure out

That what I'm saying now
You'll realize what it's all about.
So don't custom-fit me
Into roles I don't fit.
I've been through too much,
I'm worth too much
To be your experiment.
Young man I know
Older nana is more marinated,
But you're ten years too young
And not yet life educated.
I'm not one to be played with.

So, I know you thought
You were ready.
But not just chronologically,
I'm light years ahead.
And I made a vow that works.
And there's more to me
Than what's between my legs.
The truth may hurt
But you're not ready.

Every Day Is Valentine's Day

And the violin plays,
And the ribbon in the sky splays,
And my heart just raises
In praises
Of praises
Full of praises to my God,
Though it may seem odd.
He IS my rod.
My staff, my comforter.
The only One whose hand is sure
Not to allow me to be plucked away,
Washed away on sandy shores of hearsay....
I love You I love You I love You...
What more can I say?
Every day to me, for You
Is Valentine's Day
A red rose for Your sacrifice.

Another for Your blood.
A pink one for Your love.
And ohhh what a friend.
A lover, a father, a mother
And husband.
A white rose for Your sinless purity.
Another white for eternity.
And another for Your Spirit
That lives and loves through me.
Finally, a joyful rose in yellow.
I cover You risen Lord
In rose petals.
Symbolic of the fragrance of my praise,
Giving honor to where honor is due,
Oh precious, Ancient of Days......

Take Things Slow

I mean, yeah…
I know you're feeling me
And I'm really feeling you, too.
But sigh…

This whole thing just kinda gives me anxiety.
It's like sigh...ahhhh,
I don't know...
I've been here before.
And yeah, there's the initial attraction
But...what comes next?
'Ya know?
And I'm not a little girl anymore,
And you're a grown man.
And there's a lot more on the line
Than when you were in school.
"Do you like me? Circle 'yes or no.'"
I would really prefer to take things slow
And whatever that looks like

It would be much better
Than what we've done before.
So…
I love your kisses.
I wouldn't mind your touch.
But also, I want you to know that
I want to do something that will last
And not just be from last night
But the rest of my life.
And if you're not a person
Who sees beyond today,
And focus on the long-term gain
And the long goal,
Then, I think I'm the wrong girl for you
And I need to let you know.

I need to let you know
I need to let you know
That I'm more than my lips,
More than my hips
And my thighs.
I need to let you know that
That there's something deeper

Than what you see in my eyes.
I need to let you know that
I have plans.
I have goals.
I have dreams.
I need to let you know that
You've got to be willing
To play your role on the team.
I need to let you know that
What's in me is greater
Than what's in the world.
I need to let you know that
I am a Kingdom kid.
I am a child of God.
He's my Dad
And I'm His girl.
So, I need to let you know that
This swag,
This sexiness,
This soul that you feel,
It comes from Him
And He's the One
Who caused my heart to heal.

I don't want to continue
In the same cycles over and over again,
Falling down the same hole.
I hope you understand
Where I'm coming from
And let the Spirit take control.
There's more on the line here
Than just mind and body
But my soul
And yours, as well.
So, if you care about me,
Help me not to worry about
Going to Hell
By making sure to keep
Your hands to yourself.
And taking time to listen
To the words that I say,
Not just looking at my lips and hips
And how my body sways.
Because, yes, I am all woman.
I am a sensual being.
But I'm also wanting to be in love
In a relationship

With the freedom
To be me,
And to be safe spiritually,
Emotionally and mentally.
And I hope you understand
What I'm saying
Because I'd like there to be
A you and me.
I would like for that to be you and me
I would like for that to be you and me
But only time will allow us to see.

Maturity

It's a dangerous thing
When a young man sounds old.
Speech of the aged
But lacks self-control.
With maturity untested,
Responsibility divested;
Try to put a lil' weight on it.
Don't go out on a limb.
Hope you don't fall.
Pray it's no child involved.

Maturity.

Inspired by Warren & Malcolm

Won Me

You won me
Over with your intentionality
In the beginning.
You were curious
Unassuming
Investigator
Interested
Fascinated

But what happened?
Am I a caged bird now?
I sing
I'm fly
You feed
You provide
But my voice is limited
At times, you desire to shut me up
But I am
In your menagerie

In your fantasy
Of what a woman should be
And you caught me.

It was a really good trap
Poetry
Wining
Dining
Driving
To oasis places
Transparency
So it seemed...

Now that you see some of
Who I am,
Does the power intimidate you?
Though I was willing to submit it to you.
Inner smallness
Always wants more.
I've shaved my head before
To please people
And just as God is saying, *Soar*
I will not allow you

Or anyone to clip my wings
Any more.
Not even me.
I fight hard
Every day
To keep my dignity off the floor.

Love is not control.
Every human has a soul
And a will.
Can you deal with Wild Child, still?
Can you stay curious
When my question
Tests your ego?
And ask the why's
Behind what has made me
Or was your curiosity
Just to charm, control and then change me?

You won some
But you lost this one.

Stockholm Syndrome

I remember
The ripping sound
Of my panties.
I remember
Trying not to cry out
Because my son was sleeping.
I was used to this though,
Inside weeping.
Dignity lost again.
Even running down the hallway
As I said, "No."

He told me months later
After I mentioned it.
He said I wanted it.
He said I was just frontin'.
He knew I wanted it.
I said I didn't but
I guess *I* didn't matter.

And it didn't matter
Because at least
Somebody wanted me.
At first, his family accepted us.
Encouraging
My codependency,
"You're so good for him."
But he was no good for me.
More support for my son,
A pseudo-family,
More than what my church leaders
would do for holidays
and my son's sports games.
Wanted a baby with him,
So, I stayed.

In hindsight,
How twisted.
Church girl,
Full of church hurt,
But a bible study leader
That the White male leaders
Expected to fail, anyway.

That’s what
“Lusty”,
“Worldly”
Single mothers
Do anyway, right?
So, I walked proudly into church with him;
My rapist,
My missionary date.
Maybe he’d marry me someday,
And I could fit in with the church ladies,
Finally.

Though I was told
He wasn't for me,
I could never scream.
My insides wanted to be free,
Knowing that his demons
Were planning on killing me,
Planning on suffocating me
And my son’s dreams.

It took me going to jail
To get free.

Sitting in a cell for 48 hours

In Guilford County.

In a snowstorm.

On Valentine's Day.

Heaped with shame.
Heaped with blame.
Regretting.
Yearning for acceptance.
Rushing towards Pharisees
Saying, "Sinners have souls, too, Daddy."

Yup, it's us,
In James 1:27,
The ones with "daddy issues"
That need the most covering
Because the wolves come
And drag us and our lambs away
While you're worried about
Who's coming to church late.

So, I stayed a year with a man
Who had a poor mental state
And our first dates ended in rape.
I think they call that Stockholm syndrome…
But I'm sharing this
To let you know you're not alone.

Love For Sale

A penny for your thoughts,
A nickel for your kiss.
A dime if you tell me, you love me;
Why is my love always for sale?

I think how I've been waiting to exhale,
Thinking how I fell
Again, in love with the idea of being wanted,
Not rejected.
Even if neglected,
I'm there.
He's there.
In the same room.
Face to the tube.
But at least he wants me there...
I guess...

Always playing Momma bear
'Cuz Papa bear's not there.

Carrying around the cares
Like I'm doing the world a favor!
But isn't it a sin to love yourself?
Poor, pious me,
Paying massage to envy me
As he touches me legally
With no tricks up his sleeves
For once.
In this case with a man, there's some trust.
Minus the lust-
There's still bucks
Involved...

A penny for your thoughts,
A nickel for your kiss.
A dime if you tell me, you love me;
Why is love always for sale?

Lord, take away these daddy issues.
Puffs Plus with Vicks rub
Won't be enough to
Catch all these tears falling,
As I keep coughing,

Choking on the thought this
Is happening, again.

A penny for your thoughts,
A nickel for your kiss.
A dime if you tell me, you love me;
Why is my love always for sale?

Then, I think about the One
Who was impaled
On a cross.
The only begotten Son
Died to wash away all my sin,
Past, present and future.
He is the most eligible suitor
Who was willing to pay more than I'm worth
Even when I don't put Him first.
He knew me since birth,
Acquainted with my sorrows on this earth.

I said Jesus,

A penny for Your thoughts,

A nickel for Your kiss.
A dime if You tell me, You love me.

He said, "Nah, keep the change.
The price has already been paid
To prove to you how much I love you.
Like Maxwell, you don't have to wonder.
For you, I rose.
For you, I went under
Into the grave.
My thoughts for you innumerable,
My ardor, My passion for you, consumable.
I've always got My eye on you.
You've got My full attention.
Between My Father and Me,
You're always in My mentions.

Stop carrying what you did yesterday.
It's forgiven.
I'm risen and still living.
Do cast your cares on Me.
I can be trusted
I've got you, full custody."

Safe

You're the guy
That I don't mind
Undressing me
With your eyes.
You're secure
When they flirt.
I am yours
And you are mine
Committed
Until the end of time.

You make me feel so fine.
I feel safe in your arms.
It wasn't like that
With so many other guys.
They wanted a piece,
But not the whole.
They wanted gratification
In their hold;
I'd feel so alone,

Dismembered.
Wanting my body
And just a piece of that,
But not my soul,
The magnificence
Of my presence.
Yet, they wanted control.

Even a child knows
When she's just a means
To an end.
Even a dog knows
When you're not his
Best friend.
But I am wanted.
From my head to my toes,
From my mind,
To my goals,
To my heart,
To my nose,
In between my thighs,
The twinkle in my eyes,
The moans and sighs,

The tears at night,
The loud laughter,
The angry silence…
I am safe in your heart.
I am cherished like fine art,
Protected by your jealous
Security.
Not altered, just vaulted.
Lovingly protecting
God's masterpiece.
I am safe.

Fly High!

(Grappling with Abandonment, Poem to My First Love)

This is how I show you that I love you...
I let you go.
Fly high!
Be great!
And here's how!
Be you!
Do you!
I'll be just fine...

If you want to leave.
Then you were never mine.
I wish you the best.
I'll even suggest
What to wear to your next date.
Don't come back
'Cuz tomorrow might be too late

If you love me,
You'd wait.
But I guess I'm not good enough
Not to wait for
But...
I guess it was lust.
Didn't know the differ-unce
'Til I got older.
Never fall for that again...
Or did I?

So, fly high.
Best goodbyes.
No, don't send
The 2nd wedding invite.
I guess you were never mine.
And that's fine.
Fly high!

What You've Done

You may not hear a Christian woman
Openly say this but
I guess I'm that one…
Your kisses make me want to
Take my
Own clothes off.
But before you touched anything,
This is what you've done.

You called me while I was working,
Listened to me vent about my day.
Had me laughing so hard
I was crying.
Saying, "Jesus take the wheel,
I can't see!
Are you praying?!"

Let's back it up a bit
What about the morning text?
The one, not stereotypical,

Not like a cut-n-paste.
But a sincere,
Good morning, Beautiful
In your own special way.

As your wedded wife,
Kisses in the morning.
Kisses goodnight.
Massaging my feet.
Moving my hair away from my face.
And so patient with me,
Making me feel secure.
And my words, my heart
And my body are in a safe place.

Protection, safety- spiritually and physically;
Mental, emotional and financial stability.
That's what a woman needs
Before you even touch her.
Then the rest, when the lights go out,
Is history.

To think, Eve made a mistake
Because of what the seducer said.

Do you hear me?
Do you love what I care about?
So how you make me feel
In word and deed
Is what determines the heat in bed.
So much differently,
Than what music and adult videos show.
It's so much deeper yet simpler
Than what the world lets us know.
Can you allow me to be strong?
Be who I am?
Can I not shame you,
Constantly reminding you when you're
wrong?
These are the little things
That make passionate nights last long.
Beyond what we've heard in songs.

You touch me from the inside
By what I hear you say.
I show you that you are respected and wanted
By how I look for you each day.

Our Playful List

Our playfulness
Our playlists…
Notes & strokes
Of the strings
As our hearts sing
In unison,
Sometimes 3-part harmony;
Yes, God is pleased
With our intimacy.
Matrimony.
Our connection runs so deep.
Simmering in the soul
And bubbling forth
On the lips,
From the hips,
On the sheets.
Music.
Is it grinding
Or dancing?

Fingertips prancing,
Tap dancing
Down your spine.
My Baby is fine!
And he's ALL mine!

Music in our bedroom so sacred,
Cords and covers so naked.
I don't want a melody
To remind you of her
Or it to remind me of he.
Just you.
And the joy we bring.
Just us two,
Making memories.
You loving me
And I loving you.
Not always a smacking,
Flipping and rubbing it down
Like hormonal teens,
But your hand behind my head
As I grip the sheets,
On my back kissing me,

Cassandra
Or Sinatra crooning
As love flies us
To the moon and back.

That's melodic,
Methodic,
God-given pleasure
Without measure.
With you,
I am home.
Safe and settled
As we love from the soul
Eternally,
Mentally,
Emotionally,
Spiritually
And physically,
Rhythmically
Ebbing
And flowing
Like the tides
From the insides.

Me on yours.
You in mine.
You in mind
On our playful list.

Intimate Simplicity

Years ago, I renamed myself
A hopeful romantic.
I know he's out there
Looking for me.

Let me tell you
What I've learned
While I'm waiting…

Not only do I have an imagination
To write this lovely poetry,
It is also to imagine
With my intellect
Manifesting some of
His deepest fantasies.

Why not?
We'd be married.
He'll never want to go

Anywhere else,
I bet ya that.
I'll tell anyone,
I wasn't born speaking in tongues!

I've learned that
The most magical sex
Is the one so free.
No one guilty
And we're not disappointing
The One we love so dearly.
The love that's built on
True intimacy.
A foundation of friendship
Where I know you
Spiritually, mentally and emotionally,
Well before physically.
Knowing you'd go to bat for me
And I'd do anything
To see you succeed.

At just the thought,
I feel relief

Because it's so much simpler
Than music taught me.
So much more sensual
Than religiosity.
So much closer to how
Our Creator created it to be.
Me wanting to give the best to you
And you wanting to give the best to me.

In Love

Rather let it be the hidden person of the heart, with the incorruptible beauty of a gentle and quiet spirit, which is very precious in the sight of God. As Sarah obeyed Abraham, calling him lord, whose daughters you are if you do good and are not afraid with any terror.

- 1 Peter 3:4, 6

Quiet and peaceable;
The Lord is so sweet to me.
He sweeps me off my feet.
Brings me to my knees.
I'm thankful for His righteousness
Because His heart I want to please.
The testimonies He gives me
Are our sweet memories.

How He's provided for me and my seed.
He's never lied to me.
The Bible says,

He's called "Faithful and True."
The One always there for you.
My forever friend.
He places me at the top.
My cup runs over
In abundance, I lend.
On Him, I depend,
To live, move and have my being.
His love is so freeing.
More than any human being.

His blessings overtake me!
I can't believe what I am seeing,
What I'm feeling.
Words cannot describe.
I feel ALIVE with Jesus!
More than those other guys!

With Christ,
My soul flies!
Plunges deep into the Spirit,
Baptized by His fire!

I’m alive y’all!

Fresh out the grave!

Living in His glory days.

I am His & He is mine.

He’s thinking of me

All the time!

I'm in love!

I Belong to You

I matter.
My voice matters.
I am wanted.
I belong to you.

I am called by your name.
I am not left wondering,
Wandering like a woman in the night.
Someone wants me home.
Someone wants me safe.
Someone cares where I am.
Someone cares where my emotions stand.
Someone wants to see me happy.

Weh dayum…
What dat feel like???
It feels like you.
Finally…
You care about my whereabouts.

You care about my doubts.
I am accepted as yours.
A part of your sheepfold
That you must protect
And provide joy for.

Wow, what a feeling!

I belong to you!

Family Tree

Some call it a village.
Some call it a tribe.
The most amazing and catastrophic thing is
it shapes how you see you inside.
It's family,
our story of origin.
Where most of life begins,
if we have them,
even in dysfunction.

My Dreams Vs. His Dreams

Almost an empty nest now...
What should I do?
Book a cruise to Europe.
Daydreams packed like the Louvre.
Marry a Greek god,
Body like marble.
Long last name like
Antetokounmpo.
Shop in Paris and grow
Old, teachin' the Cha Cha Slide
Slow tempo
With some Italian old folks.
But I love kids.
Love family.
Going after all that
God promised me,
Even if it sounds crazy.

My daydreams can wait...

Or change
To a family affair
Beaches vs. Sandals
Lord, take me there!

Mind Numbing Distractions

She taught me how to play these games
Mind numbing distractions
I learned how to escape
Mind numbing distractions

Not giving a gaze to your reactions
Stuck in the matrix
Unable to make traction
Unable to escape my dissatisfaction
Hours drift away
Numbing the pain
Like sand slipping through my fingers
Not making traction
Don't want to feel another reaction
So, I'll remain entertained
With mind numbing distractions.

Double Entendre

(Mental Health)

Stop doing that!
I wish I could tell you
How much it hurts!
I wish I had the words
To say,
Consider me first.

Sounds selfish, yes.
But I'm the one getting the calls.
I'm the one picking everything up
When the chips fall.
"Hi, Ms. Wells?
"Yes..."
"Um, we have your mother here...
She was found..."

...long pause in eternity

Is it my worst fear?
How do I manage 50-year old
Responsibilities in my 20 years?
Who do I call?
What does life look like next?
I don't even have a key
To her apartment...

"...Ms. Wells?
Are you still there?"
"Yes, I'm here."
"Yes, she's in St. Raphael's Hospital
And is spending a few days here.
Do you know her meds?
Can you bring some clothes?
What's her insurance info?"

"Mom, can we go play?"
"Hold on,
I'm on the phone babe..."

"Ms. Wells, she's on
The 2nd floor

Room 202.
Do you have any questions?"

"No, thank you..."
I hang up
Without a moment
To consider
What to do.
I've got to take care
Of my mini-me
And go see about you.

Now that's selfish
To rob a 20-something year old
Of her youth,
Catering to you
While trying to rear her child, too.
No childhood for me
Not in the 10's
Nor the 20's
But our family,
Your siblings,
Won't acknowledge

What your choices
Took from me.

It came to the point
When I'd receive these calls
Over 10 years,
I'd always expect the worst.
So, when the final call came,
It was already rehearsed.
In shock but duty,
I took my first breath.
Then sucked it up
Like a big girl
To honor your death.

To this day
Except in counseling,
No one knows the depth
Of this pain.
And I still don't know
It all,
It's so deep.
And I'm writing this

Not to undo
The honor I gave you.
But to help someone else through
The double entendre
Of loving and honoring elders
Whose decisions dishonor you.

If I could love you all over again,
I'd set better boundaries
And let your siblings take on more.
If I knew what I know now,
I wouldn't have had to be so strong.
This way, I could love you
For who you are
And not expect
You to be the mom
I needed.

Instead of our differences,
Focusing on what
We did agree upon.
To accept you where you are,
Even though you didn't

Understand me.
What family couldn't see,
I'd get help from NAMI.
If I knew it existed...

Hindsight is 20/20.
In grief, it's called "bargaining,"
Wishing you could
Change the outcome
After loss...
So, I'm not beating
Myself up.
There's so much wisdom
I've gained.
If it weren't for you,
I wouldn't be in the Faith.
Because of the cards dealt,
I'm a better mom,
A better person.
I've learned that
What I eat,
What I do,
Where I go,

Affects another person.
So, I need to take care of myself.
It's not fair to the next generation
To do what I want to do
And let them pay for it.

I've learned that
Not everyone has
The perfect parent story.
That it's MY story
And it's all for God's glory.
No shade to my parents or family,
But children have to
Be able to
Share our truths, too.
Shed light on the shame
In the dark;
Let guilt go!
So, we can move
Onto the new.
Honor is important,
But healing
And helping others is, too.

So, if you've felt abandoned,
Mismanaged,
This poem is for you!
If God can see me through,
He'll do it for you, too!
The Double Entendre.

Double Entendre Part II (Bloody Love?)

Blood was everywhere.
I don't even remember the sound.
For weeks after nose surgery,
Her nose stayed bloody
And gauze bound.
I just remember the next time.
Though I was nine,
There was an argument.
I needed to intervene.
Counselor Tamika at 10,
Holding him back from getting his gun,
Sitting on his lap discussing,
Calming him down,
Giving instructions,
While telling my mom to "Shut up."

It was always in the kitchen

The same place where
"Family Life Today"
Would play from the radio
On the washing machine.

He busted her nose.
The man who helped me
Learn my daily words
Since first grade.
"Wolf, w-o-l-f, wolf."
Words in a Ziploc baggie
As we sat in the living room.
My childhood protector;
Taught me how to fight
Stand up for myself,
Was the same man
Putting his hands on my mom
Those many nights.

But he was drunk, though.
Only happened around the holidays
When he mixed light and dark liquor.
Though, he was a Romanoff Vodka

Kinda guy day to day.
I remember the tinkling of glass bottles
In the vinyl dirty clothes bin
And all the places he hid the evidence.
But he was my childhood friend,
My protector,
My "kick 'em in the nuts"
Street instructor.
Vietnam war vet,
My step dad, Kenny.

So, when my husband hit me,
I was in complete shock.
The first thing that came to mind was…
"If my nose is broken,
I'm going to kill him."
And it happened in the kitchen,
Again.
My son was about the same age as me
How could this happen?
He was bleeding profusely.
I'd learned from my mom
And her friends growing up,

When fighting a grown man use a key
Or something sharp.
My eye was black just like hers
And she was no longer living.
My son didn't stand in the middle, like I did.
But yes, we were all in the kitchen.
How did this happen?
And it happened again...
Just someone else different.

They say that we have a list
Of our ideal mate,
But our subconscious
Has a whollllle other plan!
Which is very frustrating when
You're a good girl
Like my mom was,
But you keep attracting a broken man.
Then,
You imitate the same cycles
In front of your son,
Praying he never hurts or beats anyone.
Or falls in love with someone

With poor mental health
And addictions.
Because our subconscious mind
Is trying to recreate the trauma
From Momma
To reverse the pain of the past
In a new situation
By attracting a similar scenario
Of an enabler and addict,
Or codependent and abuser;
To cancel out the past pain
But only reinforcing the cycle
Over and over and over again.

It's a double entendre.
I want the right person in
But I can't get this fatal attractor out.
So, we stay perpetually single
Or our relationships carry a cloud.
But I'm out!
I'm in therapy!
I'm in tapping and coaching
And doing deep, deep, deep soul searching.

And learning about what makes me happy,
And boundaries, boundaries, boundaries!
I will free my stuck inner child
So my subconscious will stop being
The epitome of insanity.
No more ignoring red flags.
Trust my gut.
That there's nothing,
Absolutely nothing wrong with me.
No more shame!
That my past is my past
And I hold the pen
To rewrite my destiny!

Double Entendre

Part III

(The Miscarriage?)

He has the potential to
Murder you,
To set you back from
How far you've gotten to.
But that urge to miss him,
To stay and make a life,
To be a foolish man's wife
Won't go away.

"I must be crazy.
What's wrong with me?"
Says the shame of loving a man so
dangerously.
Why don't I love myself
Enough to let go?

To trust the whispers in my soul,
It's safe to let go.

I lost the baby.
The final tie
He had to me,
Or is it?
I love his mom dearly
And he knows it,
Using her as an avenue
To stay close.
Desiring to mourn collectively
With her and the kids,
But risk being confronted
By him.

How did I get here?
Torn and still grieving alone?
When does this pain end?
I thought I saw a rainbow.
I thought a new family began.
Laying here as kittens,
Try to lick away my tears.

No hugs, popcorn, movies,
Crying with tissues on the couch.
Cuddled with a mom's comfort
After the news of the child,
The hope is completely bled out.

And at the same time,
Praise God for a new beginning,
Right?
My body helped me avoid
A lifetime tragedy.
It removed & recovered
Miraculously!
No medical intervention needed.
I'm alive.
I'm well.
And I'm physically able to do what is needed.

So, it's a sweet & sour
Kinda day.
A hand-raised,
Tears-streaming praise
That I could keep secret

The rest of my days
If I didn't share this
Miscarriage with you.
This unwedded mother
Openly honestly
Disclosing to you
The mixed emotions
Of repeating childhood trauma
While being saved
And still thanking the Lord
For His life He gave
To pay the price for my mistakes.
Though, it still hurts very deeply,
It's a cost of sin.
It's a cost of being human.
No one ever said deliverance
Was beautiful.
I'm sad and feeling hopeless again,
At the same time grateful,
Freed from an abuser, once again.

Not Abandoned

(Father's Day Tribute)

Tamika,
Tamiko,
Tanika.
What lovely names.
"People child" and her sisters
From foreign lands.
Black lives paid
To save people.
Yet, in his country,
He wasn't equal.
In Jim Crow South,
It was clear:
National terrorism
Didn't want him here.
My dad,
Unwanted, disrespected
But expected
To kill innocent blood

For a nation
That didn't value him
To begin with.

Many nights, my dad spoke
Vietnamese in his sleep.
Medicating,
Blowing O-rings.
Too bruised
And dejected
To be a responsible father
Of a daughter.
So, I was raised by my mother.
Especially, when they found
My dad in the streets with me
Late nights
While she was working 3rd.
They said he was a nodder…

I remember the night
When a man wanted to
Take me home to his "wife and kids"
Which I'm not sure really existed...

As drunk and high
As my dad was,
He wouldn't let me go.
I remember at three years old
Being the center
Of a tug of war.
But as drunk and as high
As he was, my father
Wouldn't let me go!

So, I say to those
Feeling abandoned,
Those of us feeling neglected
By things we cannot see,
By parents, forsaken
Not everything in life is fair.
But it is my prayer
We all make it
To the point where
We find some good
Out of jacked-up situations.
As an adult now,
I know it wasn't all his fault

I was abandoned.
He fought the best he could,
Demons from a war
In a country
In which he shouldn't have landed.
Let MLK Jr. tell it!
My dad should be here
Able to raise a daughter
And know he's not abandoned.

Dear Family…

My one desire was to grieve with you
But every time I looked up from my tears,
You were gone.
And off in your spouses' arms.
Must be nice
While I had to stay strong
Alone for my son.

I was socially distanced
Twelve years before 2020.
This year showed me
Everything I've ever been through
Was never wasted,
But prepared me for today.
Queen of holding spaces,
To continue to show up for you
Even in uncomfortable places,
Even if I'm standing alone.
To hold my own

And know I'm never alone.
And also, when I need to be weak,
I will and stay home
Alone. To cry. To sort. To sing. To shout.
I will not take this pain to the grave.
I'm letting it out!

I've learned that
Help doesn't always come
From flesh and your own blood.
2020 wasn't all my own color
Nor denomination,
But all from God's beloved creation
And I'm OK with that.

Like life,
2020 has confirmed that
Whatever you do have
Is all you need,
And all you lost was never needed.
So, grieve healthy
But don't look back.

God knows the plan.
I can't grow staying in my own clan
But I'm writing this
To express something
I didn't have the words to say.
You left me hanging
But I'm going to be ok.
All I can do is pray,
Get support elsewhere,
And love you anyway.

Dear family…

Tamika "People Child" Wells

What's it like to be a People Child?
To be me.
Loved by many,
Fully known by only
One.
Belonging in limited,
Temporary,
Shifting places.
Recognized,
Admired by many faces.
Holidays for decades,
Never the same place.
A family of my own,
Long gone.
Orphaned wanderer,
Yet adopted into the Beloved
In Heaven

But watching others enjoy
On Earth,
What I used to take for granted.
Working extra hard,
Being intentional to rebuild
The types of relationships
That truly satisfy,
Not just hold a place
In the empty spaces
Of my personal life,
While people see the success
Only from the outside.

It's lonely being an only child,
Being your only safety.
Accepting who I have become now,
Forgiving my younger self
And learning to trust me again,
My wise upbringing,
My intuition.
Able to make others smile.
Eating at restaurants alone,
Surviving on my own.

Ignoring past shadows of
What could be
And what was…
Giving thanks for everyone
That has come
And gone
From my life.
That's what it's like…
Right now,
Being a People Child.
Still being able to smile,
Light up a room.
Be a boss
When others don't know the cost
Of my oil.
Being ok being misunderstood,
Like my mother, honest and loyal.
Being too much
When you're up close.
Seeing the scars
And the flaws.
A mosaic
Of good & bad.

Beautifully painful
And will always be like that.
Because the trauma
Has helped me
Become who I am.
I am of substance,
I am of strength.
I'm valued by me
Before you.
Compassionate,
Nonjudgmental,
At heart, still wild
I'm People Child.

Emotions

Emotions,
indicators that you are alive.
Let's sit with them,
but don't lock them in the trunk
and don't let them drive.

Xylophone

Ups & downs like a xylophone,
Dealing with emotional
High & lows,
It's not something we always disclose
Like a cat with a canary
In its mouth.
Muffling, *I'm fine…*
Fake smile.
Even a laugh,
But we keep going;
Anxiety boiling inside.

Thoughts rushing,
Perusing the halls
Of our memory banks.
Halls of terror.
Halls of joy.
Halls of laughter.
Halls of pain.

Trying to forgive
Ourselves.
Let live
Or never relive again.
But they come like waves
Throughout each day.

Was never taught in Pre-K
That this was normal.
The tears were hushed
Or frowned upon,
Especially if they seemed
"Unreasonable."
Be strong!
Suck it up!
An employer told me once…
Put your big girl panties on!
But…
But..
My grandma just died…

Self-regulated
Medicated

Or meditated
Or prayed it
Or Shyt!
Do all three!!!
But only me
Is going to take care of me.
Only I hear the thoughts in my head.
Only I know the dreams
That wake me from my bed.
Get out of your head,
They said,
But where else do I be?
Living from the heart
Isn't what pays the bills
In our society.
So it seems…

As I express
And not repress,
Not suppress
But paint
And style,
Smile and invent,

As I boundary
And border
My sacred spaces
With beautiful gates,
Build supports
And speakers
For my sounds to resonate,
I ripple and effect
These beautiful souls
Around me,
As we see,
As we sing together
In harmony.

Because we're made a masterpiece.
A master symphony
And this cacophony
Is normalcy.
I accept all of me,
No judging
The highs or the lows.
It's the human experience
And I'm grateful for each of those.

We share, we connect
Thanks to all these notes
On our emotional xylophone.

I Have No Words

Give me time to contemplate
Emotions that resonate
In my soul,
In my mind
But I...
As eloquent as I am...

I have no words...

They call it
Emotional overwhelm.
My fight, flight or freeze
Mechanism wants to take over me
But I know it's not healthy
So
Just let me be
As I dismantle this storm
Of feelings
Desiring to take over me.

I don't want to react
Haphazardly,
So please.
I beg of you,
Let me be.

Because I have no words...

The air has been
Sucked out of me.
My senses
Are in a flurry.
I don't want to be in a hurry
Which will do more harm
Than good.
I know you want to be understood.
I do too
Without my response being twisted.
Give me the respect
I'm giving

Because I have no right words

For you.
My sensibilities are offline.
But with a little space...
A little time...
We'll be just fine.

When I find my words.

A Full So Empty

We are not designed to live in "I"
Our DNA says "We"
Meaning family.
Meaning community.
It's no wonder we
Medicate.
We meditate
On social media
To hide the pain.
Disembodied souls
Without a home,
Where ME becomes WE.
Where YOU
And I
Become US.
A safe place
For we to rest.
A place where you and I are known,
That place where we belong.

There's a difference
In a soul
With and without a purpose,
With and without a home.
I made my purpose you
But now it's just me.
Searching, sighing
Trying to settle
In an abode to call home
Without you.
Uncertainty and ambiguity
Gripping me.

The billboards of their faces
Say "Get over it."
"Pray about it."
"I'm ok,
You should be, too."
Their songs sing...
"Be strong."
"This too shall pass."
And yeah and "I need you
To do *this* and do *that*" for me,

But you and I are not we.
As they walk hand in hand
As we.
Not me.
Not I.
Just us.

Where is the justice?
In giving your all
For someone
You have to give away, eventually?
And live without community?
No one prepared me for this,
Though I tried to prepare you
To fly
High and strong.

Though I was your strength,
My strength has become yours.
But I feel like you hate me for it.
Waiting for the day
When you see that
The last 20

Was all about you;
There was no me.

Like the architect
Of the Twin Towers,
Staring at an empty hole
Of what used to be,
I'm picking up the pieces
Of what's left of me.
I know she's there,
Looking through unpacked boxes
And closets
Of what was needed then
But not now.
Who's here to help me
Make sense of a full,
So empty?

I just want to walk away from it all.
Throw it all away,
Burn it all down.
It was ours.
It fit us

But not this me.
And here I am,
In my tears,
With two hands
To do all this by myself
Once again.
And I'm tired.
I gave all my strength away
Like The Giving Tree,
With soil
Eroding from up under me.
What you see
Is a shell of the vibrant me.

Hiding in one of these,
Some of these boxes,
Somewhere...
I don't know,
Searching for a purpose,
A sense of meaning
Beyond myself again.
To rebuild a new beginning
Beyond what was.

Breadcrumbs

A cat drops a turd
On your nightstand
And runs.

Don't just clean it up
And chastise him.
Check the litter box
Did you clean it?

What's the why?

Our bodies give us
Breadcrumbs
To solve malfunctions.

Our emotions give us
Breadcrumbs
To solve malfunctions.

If I'm feeling or reacting
Out of my usual,
What's the why?

If he's feeling or acting
Out of his usual,
What's the why?

Let's dig deeper.

Ministry?

If we can't be tender
To somebody's tears,
Then why are we in ministry????
The devil this
And the devil that…
Some things are our
Human ignorance
And we keep blaming him for that!

What is the driving force
When genuine emotions
Are disregarded?
Have we become stonyhearted,
Mindless of others' tears?
Others fears
That they don't just get over
In one night?
Someone just died!
Wake up!
She's probably not

Sleeping well at night!
And it's been a year,
Yes, but grief never leaves you
Right away.
It never leaves you quite
The same.

The devil, the devil
The devil is destroying,
We cry
While we're chewing
On each other,
Comparing ourselves
To what another
Is or isn't doing.

Railroading peoples' pleas
To breathe,
All for the need for control.
That's narcissistical
When people are used as
The end to your means.

And Holy Spirit
Can teach you that.
Get the education;
In all thy getting,
Get understanding!
And by all means,
PLEASE get therapy!
Because what's emotionally
Driving you
Is trying to drive me.
And it's not the gentle quiet
Holy Ghost.
You *won't* push me.
And God knows…

At this time
When so many people
Are hurting,
With all due respect,
I don't care about
Your position.
I don't have capacity
To do crazy

When people are
Hurting and dying.
Drama is draining
And your tone
Needs home training.

You can't blame
The devil
When you don't know
How to talk to me.
And you're in ministry,
Intimidating people
Like you're fresh
Off the streets.

You can win more bees
And friends with honey
Than with vitriol,
Gossip and acting funny.
That's the flesh
Doing the devil's job
And nothing can be received
Of God

Carnally.

P.S. don't go digging
In my closet, things
I've confessed to you
As a person of prayer,
My dry bones,
My sins, nailed to the cross
To make your insecurities
Feel better.
It makes you no better
Than a scarlet letter
Washed off in the rain
By His blood stains
And adds up to
The things you
As a leader
Will answer to God for.
I pray if this is the case,
God have mercy…
On you.

Sad Day

It's Sad Day.
A day when I'm not ok.
Never knew it was ok
To feel this way,
And it's Sad Day.
Y'all ok?
'Cuz I'm not ok
Today.

Let me lay
In my bed
With the covers over my head.
Let me stay in my office,
Answer a couple calls
If I can…
Warning:
I may be irritable…
Let me go home.
Let me stand

In the shower
For hours
Crying
Because it's the most natural place
For me
To shed my tears
Away; a way
I don't have to answer.
I don't have to talk through
When I'm not ready.
A place where I don't have to be strong,
Solving your problems while I'm limping.
A place where I don't have to be heady
Or weighty and perfect.
A place just to sit
And cry in my humanness.
A place where humans
Feel most vulnerable, literally.
Emotionally allowing myself
To be
Free,
To be hurting,
To be full of sorrow

Until I'm empty.
Unashamed that I'm frail right now
And still beloved,
As I sink in the tub,
Head just above water
Until these waves of tears pass.

Then I'll arise in strength
After this emotional purging,
Giving into the urgings
To hope again.
But THIS time,
I won't railroad Sad
And pretend to be Glad,
Or turn to default Mad
Or Blame
Or Reasoning,
Maybe later,
But not today,
Because it's Sad Day.

A day of recovery
For my heart and soul.

Willing to lose all control
As I fall into the arms of sorrow.
Not willing to do anything terminal
Or permanent.
Let these tears be my medication.
Let these cries empty me out!
Bottles consumed
Can't reverse the gloom.
Let me scream!
Let me dance!
Let me shout!
With you,
If you are safe to.
But addiction
Will cause me to revisit
Double this affliction.
No matter how far I run,
The answer is so simple,
Though walking through pain
Isn't fun.

But knowing this message of Sad
Is Heaven sent.

A trimming of dead
Emotional leaves
Or saying goodbye to a season
Or people that no longer suit me,
Though I felt so comfortably
Settled in he or she and we.
Mourning the hope
Of a new life.
A time to finally fit in with
New moms,
New spouses,
Buying houses,
Looking for baby seats,
Planning…
Enjoying retirement together,
Not fighting the cancer
She didn't beat.

Feeling like a failure.
Looking for answers, again
Eventually…
But today,
I offline my mind

And lean into my heart,
Pour out my soul
Whether in a group
Or alone,
Safe to be vulnerable,
I will cling to the hope of love
One more time or two today,
Bask in deep sorrow
And then let you go…

Initially,
Sad day may be weeks;
It may be months,
Flickering off and on
At the slightest thought
Or memory.
Then one day,
It'll be a day or two throughout the years
As we love on.
As we live on
And open our hearts
Again, and again.

Sad day is a place
When we see others mourn.
We recall the memories
And extend a tissue,
Remembering what you went through
And knowing the fragility of life
Standing before you.
Even if they appear strong.
Taking Sad Days produces
Compassion,
Willingness to take helpful
Empathetic action.
Knowing you can't take away
Their pain
But you can make their day.
Make the interaction as comforting
And peaceful as possible
For the next human.
So, take a Sad Day.
Lean into sorrow
And be ok tomorrow.
But today is Sad Day
And it's OK…

Lessons from Anger

Anger is an indicator
Of fear or pain.
It says, "I'm afraid."
It says, "I won't get played!"
It says, "I'm tired of being humiliated.
Over and over and over again."
It may even say,
"Since you didn't do something to protect me,
them, us,
I will!
This is my warning
Like a dog barking.
Whether loud, passive
Or growling…
BACK UP!
Or there will be
Consequences to pay!"

Everyone looks for the crown fires.

The things they can see,
But there's so many angry people
Who manage it passively.
They deny they have an anger problem.
Though it comes out in withdrawal
Of affection or sarcasm.
They are seething, smoldering,
Hoping you feel their pain.
Like a kettle about to whistle,
But they were taught
It's not proper to set boundaries
By saying what you ought to.
That's passive anger.
You know the quiet Mother in the church
Who put everyone first,
Though her feelings are hurt?
Stuffing down pain,
Until it manifests as dis-ease.
We can pray and release
But we also have to know
How to confront things tactfully.

And there's me…

The potential hot head
Going off in the drive thru.
"How many times do I have to tell you???
More cream and sugar!
Ahora dame crema y azúcar!!!!"
Fighting off high blood pressure
At a young age
Because I've been pushed around
In life since I was young.
I've had as much as I can take.
Pilfered, molested, neglected, raped…
We don't know his story.
We don't know her case.

And to think,
With today's technology,
We should know each other
More intimately.
Hopefully, in a safe place.
But we talk at each other,
Envy each other's highlight reels,
Desperately needing a safe space
To be human, naked and unashamed

Without it going viral.
Or we're entitled,
Thinking lasting fulfillment comes easy.
Frustrated when the fairy dust
Wears off, feeling empty.

So, we vent!
Lose it!
Tell it like it is!
Burning bridges,
Smacking bishes.
Then wondering can
We still be friends?
What do you mean
There's no more wedding?
And healthy people
Won't put up with it.
And healthy people are who
We desire to attract.
Then we've got to learn to
Respond and not react.
These cycles are vicious.
So, we've turned to yoga,

To workouts,
To online shopping,
Eating to find inner peace,
When a safe conversation
Or conversations
Will give so much clarity.
Whether in counseling,
Safe tribes,
We need to bounce our ideas and fears.
Or spiritual connection
In prayer, knowing someone cares.
But feeling like there's no hope,
Feeling like we have to fight,
Take flight or freeze,
Or placate and people-please:
Are these
Symptoms of a dis-ease?
We're lonely.
Feeling misunderstood and unhelped
And we have to fight for survival
All by ourselves.
That's what the inner child remembers
But today, it isn't true.

Look up, all around you;
We're here to help you through.

Anger management class taught me that
I'm a Truth Speaker
But just because I'm a rescuer
Doesn't mean I have to jump in
The tomb either.
My instructor taught,
We know what dead things smell like.
We know trouble.
Speak your truth to Lazarus.
Hopefully, he'll listen to you,
But keep it moving.
Or they'll trap you in their prison.
Don't let people unwilling to change,
Change you.
My prayer now is,
Lord, is this for me to do?

So, I've learned this
After taking Anger Management twice.
Once for me, once for my son.

Yes, he's a son of a gun!
But I learned that those mechanisms
Got me this far
But they aren't useful where I'm going.
I won't let past behaviors
Limit the opportunities
Of where I am going.
And instigators who see my potential
Will try to trip me up;
Push my buttons.
But what if there's nothing,
No more triggers for them to touch?

I use pain & pissitivity
As the symptoms that they are.
Get the tapping, if I can,
Redirect my circuits,
Guard my heart
Because temptations will come.
But evil, you might win some,
But you just lost one!
Today I choose to build bridges
And have less fear of burning some.

What If I Write?

What if I write?
Poems, soliloquies
Effervescent psalms
Hymnals, annals of songs
Full of generations
Of joy and of pain.
What if I write?

Love songs
Lyrics
Prose
Not so composed
As the stoic militant
Face you see.
What if I write?

Eloquent scripts
Full of magic
Mystics

Make you sick
To know you passed this face by
Without a blink of an eye
Not knowing I
Was a journalist
Documenting the dancing
Of your soul.
What if I write?

Ideas that were founded
In the heavens.
Author's name not given
But lessons worth living.
What if I write?

The dissertation
That delivers you from poverty
Develops your artistry
Molds and shapes pottery
With the flick of my stylus
Like the breath in my lungs
Rhythmic like capoeira drums.
What if I write?

Help! Somebody

Depressed
Can't get dressed
Stuck
Rut
Not even sorrow
Unplugged
From my emotions.
Undercurrent
Of despair.
So low of a wave
It's not easily detected
Except by experience
Or specialist.

What do I smell like?
Who cares?
No one's here.
No one cares.
Do I matter?

Why am I here?
What are these tears
Of not eating
Overeating
Not sleeping
Not moving out of bed.
Not getting out of my head.
They think I'm just lazy,
Feeling sorry for myself.
But honestly,
As motivated as I was
As I usually am,
My soul feels damp.
My soul feels camped
In a pyrex bowl.
Lid tight.
No breath.
No escape
Inside a microwave.
It's hot in here
But there's no lever
I see to get out,
Though you see it

From the outside.

But I'll kick!
I'll scream!
I'll get help!
I'm not dying!
Though my soul feels muted,
I'll keep crying!
Move my body
Until my brain follows.
This doesn't have to be my
Tomorrow.
And it won't be
But a story to
Help!!! somebody.

Good Grief

Tears, trepidation,
Shaking, holdin' onto cold hands.
No one understands
Like one who's
Buried a loved one before.
Yet, it's all different.
No one has the exact same
Sentiments.
Whether close
Or estranged,
The soul mourns the loss
Of connection,
The missing opportunity
For affection
For once…
Or again.

Bargaining…
If I just did this or that?

Give me one more chance.
It could be the loss of a dreadful job
Or relationship.
Something inside still misses it;
The routine of connection or possession.

Ever had a broken engagement?
Deep disappointment?
Left at the altar
Of life?
Missing a husband?
Missing a wife?
Life canceled by cancer?
No happy ending?
Left without answers,
Lacking motivation to move on
Though they tell you to?
But how the heck do they know
What you're going through?!

So, how could grief be good?
Why is it a part of life?
Makes no sense,

These emotional rollercoasters
Leave me feeling helpless
Like a child with no defense.
Like fighting the invisible,
If people can't see your tears,
They don't comprehend what's wrong.
It could be a flower,
A scent, color or song
That sends us into a spiral
For God knows how long…

So why is this grief so good?
Grief can tenderize the heart.
Makes us selfish humans
Come together.
We gather at funerals and weddings.
We knit our hearts back together
With compassion,
In the rain, in the pain of life.
Grief also releases the ugly.
What do you mean?
Your character is tested,
Preyed upon, played upon

At the most vulnerable times.
And it makes one wise
To the company they do
Or no longer need to keep.
Grief births a release
Of tears on a lesser occasion
We'd rather keep
To play strong.
Yet, a faucet opens up on the inside.
Good grief makes grown men cry,
Opening them up to receive empathy;
Something that's usually hard
For the strong to receive.
Good grief makes bonds stronger.
Helping us realize
Petty fights don't matter
Because we need to cherish
Who we have now.
We don't know the day or hour.
We don't know how much longer
We get to enjoy the kiss.
We don't know how many more times
We'll enjoy that favorite dish

Or when she leaves the light on.
Oh, we'll miss it.
So let bygones, be bygones...

Good grief causes us to center
On the good,
Relishing memories,
Enjoying similarities
Of how they made us
Who we are to be.

Good grief can be cathartic.
Comforting the lonely
With the right company,
Softening the most bitter.
Good grief motivates
And makes saints out of sinners.
Losers grow to winners.
"I" transforms to "we"
As empathy grows and flows
Like the sea.

Good grief!

An indicator of how deeply we love.
A reminder to stop, pause and breathe.
Good grief lasts long
But gives us hope for eternity.
That's Good Grief!

(Dedicated to Shaquille O'Neal and Michael Jordan to honor their beautiful expression of grief in the untimely passing of Kobe & Gianna Bryant)

It Ain't Over

Despair
Loss
Pains in my chest
Daggers in my back
Tremors in my breast.

My heart rate so loud
I hear it in my ears.
Tears
Stream in my heart
Because at this moment
I'm face to face with Fear
Like a dog
If I cry now
It'll know I'm weak
My kids need me
But I can't breathe.

The weight of the world

Is on my chest
But I hear a voice say
It's not over yet.

What's not over?!
You mean this never ending
Hall of horror?
Endless smoke & mirrors
Downward spirals of mess?!
That I'VE got to clean up
And no one's home yet???

I feel so alone.
I feel I've done everything wrong,
When I confide
Instead of a comforting
Supportive arm,
'Cuz Lord knows!
I can't describe what I need
Right now...
I get shut down
Misunderstood
Chastised...

So, if I could just leave.
Be with those I love
Who are already gone.
Maybe they'll miss me,
Maybe they'll see they were wrong.
Tired of standing,
Looking so strong...

And I hear it again...
It's not over yet.
Don't leave here too soon.
You're going to tell your story
And bring others through, too.
Your heart is a fountain,
A river of wisdom,
Washing away the
Mountains of your pain.
Just live through this dark hour.
You'll see light and love again soon.
It's not over!

So, I get up from this kitchen floor,
Open up the front door.

Let the light shine on my face,
Realizing even when it's cloudy,
There's a new day
If I just rise up.
Fly up, remember the hope
Of His calling…
Just then, the phone rings;
It's my friend.
She says,
"Come to prayer, Tamika.
I'm worried about you."
Go to prayer without a care.
If she didn't call,
I might not be here.
Pastor laid hands
And Suicide left.
Gone was the weight.
Gone was the pain in my chest.

My life ain't over!
Because I needed to get this message
To you!
Death said, "Lay with me."

And I almost did.
But then you wouldn’t have heard this story.
He'd have a two-fer
And you wouldn't get your breakthrough!

But your life...
It ain't over!
Your hope, it ain't over!
Your destiny, it ain't over!
Your calling, it ain't over!
Your joy, it ain't over!
Your dreams, they ain't over!
Just keep on living!
Your mourning is turning to dancing
TODAY!
Even if circumstances
Aren't changing.

It's not over!
We need you!
And you need us!
Grief is natural and real
And there's help for us!

‘Cuz it ain't over!

We have a story to tell!

It Ain't Over!!!

A Song of Surrender

Rejoice with those who rejoice, and weep with those who weep. Be of the same mind toward one another.

\- Romans 12:15-16

(Singing Chorus)

Eeeeh God Eeeh God
Eeeh God Eeeh God

Though I am slain, yet will I trust You
If I walk away, who can I run to?
The whole of my life is in Your hands
You're the Only One who understands
So, I lift my hands…and say… (sigh)

Eeeh God Eeeh God
Eeeh God Eeeh God
Eeeh God Eeeh God
Eeeh God Eeeh God

Though I am slain, yet will I trust You
If I walk away, who can I run to?
You're the Only One to see me through
So, I put my faith and trust in You

(Selah- Instrumental)

(Spoken Word)
As I look back over my life,
All the pain and all the strife,
I don't know where I'd be,
If I didn't call your name early.
Before pubescence
And late adolescence,
You remembered the covenant we made,
Though I forgot the price You paid.
And throughout 12 years of mistakes,
You endlessly forgave and forgave.
Even when I fell from my high horse,
You refused to divorce
Me, but continually wooed me,
Until I returned to your love eternally.

So, with all this in mind
The reality that You are too kind
To leave me in the midst of my pain
Helps me to keep breathing day by day.
Though there are trials I cannot explain,
To live is Christ and to die is gain.
So, all I can say is (sigh)

Ye God Ye God
Ye God Ye God
Ye God Ye God
Ye God Ye God

(Bridge)
Though I sit alone,
I'm not on my own
My hand You hold
And You reign upon the throne…So…

Ye God Ye God
Ye God Ye God
Ye God Ye God

Ye God Ye God

(Selah- Instrumental)

(Spoken Word)

People have come and people've gone
But not my will but Your will be done
This is a song of surrender
When my heart is broken and tender,
Meditating on Your Word is how I remember
All fiery darts must Return to Sender
Now, I can selflessly be a lender
A lender of all that You've given me.
Healing others and delivering from tragedy
Knowing this life is not about me.
To whom much is given, also comes great responsibility.
To use the abundance of grace towards me,
To heal the hurting humanity.
A wounded soldier arises to victory.
Just like my Savior's story in history.
(Chorus)

Faith

Faith can be our gravity;
it can also help us defy it.
It's evolved over the years,
got me through all the tears.
So glad I tried it.
Just frustrated with how man has mired it.

It is Good

When God is shared
From a masculine perspective,
People can forget the attributes
Of a caring, nurturing God.
Good shepherds are just like that.
Not like colonial influenced religion
That gets offended
When others compare Him
To a woman.
But Jesus wept.
God rejoices over us with singing,
And He quiets us with His love.
He saw each day of creation
And exclaimed, “It was good.”
Or “It was very good.”
All expressions of emotions.

Sanitizing scripture,
Making God sound like
He's saying, *Get over it.*

When He tells Joshua
To take the Promised Land,
Doesn't expound on the fact
That they mourned for 30 days.
And in some Jewish traditions,
They mourn a loved one for a year.

God has emotions.
He understands our emotions.
He holds space for us daily
And we should do the same.
We are made in His image and likeness.
There's nothing masculine or feminine
About emotions because we all have them.
That's how we were created and
It is GOOD!!!

When He Came Into My Life

Repent therefore and be converted, that your sins may be blotted out, so that times of refreshing may come from the presence of the Lord.
Acts 3:19

Since Jesus came into my life
Yes, it's obvious He's changed me.
People always say,
"The Lord has rearranged me!"
But I feel you deserve more than a cliché.
So, I open my heart and share
Some of the deepest parts within.

When I was livin' in sin,
My will, my way, seemed right.
I ignored stop signs, hunger pains,
And even ran a few red lights.

I mean, if I wanted it, I grabbed it.
If I desired something in life,
I probably had it.

But still waking up
In the middle of the night, hungry.
Walking in the daylight, thirsty.
Drivin' the car of life so fast,
That, with all the windows down,
I couldn't get enough air
Then……CRASH!!!!!!!

Still ignoring the warnings,
I found myself in situations that
If I weren't so enslaved,
I would not be there.
I said, if you weren't so Enslaved,
You know, I know,
We wouldn't go there.

(Chorus)
Lord, You changed me
And rearranged me

Since You came into my life
In Christ, I have liberty
Now I am free indeed
Since You came into my life
Lord, You changed me
Rearranged me
Since You came into my life

Like water in a shattered vase,
I found myself leaking into cracks,
Into any dirty, dark place.

Then one day,
While picking up pieces
Of my broken life from the ground,
I touched His feet.
I didn't know why but
I began to weep.
My wounded soul was found.

Jesus reached down to me
As I looked up.
I gave Him my hand and

He picked me up.
He embraced me
As filthy as I was.
Washed me and healed me
With His flesh and His blood.

He showed me how He yearned for me.
He called me home,
And time and time again, I refused.
And His heart cried for me.
He showed me the way of His love
And how He died for me.
And when I thought I was alone,
He was fighting for me.
And when I was abused,
And beaten as a child,
He was there…….crying beside me.

(Chorus)

Oh, let me tell you how goooood
The Lord has been to me!!!
Since I have become His,

I'm no longer fatherless
I have a Father in Heaven
Who guards me and keeps me.
When I'm hungry, He feeds me.
When I'm thirsty, His love fills me.
My cup is overflowing!!
When I'm in my Lord's presence,
I can't stop glowing.

Everything I lost out in the world
He has restored, sevenfold.
Holidays are not even the same!
When my Lord gives back,
It's not cheap or lame.
I'm telling you, it ain't the same.
Since the day, He gave me His name,
My life has not been the same!!
I was blind, but now I see.
All things that glittered to me
Weren't gold in the world.
The clubs, the music, the clothes,
The videos, the one-night episodes…

(Chorus)

To a hungry man, even the bitter tastes sweet.
But let me tell you,
There's nothing out there that can compete!!!
There's nothing that can compare!!
I don't care what you buy.
I don't care what you try.
I don't care what you drive.
I don't care where you live.
I don't care what you lay with…
The high is temporary.
It sends you back for more.
But my God, my Father, my King, my Lord
Gives me more than I can ask for!!!

What kind of love
Lays down His life for a friend?
Friend? Your "friends"?
When the drama begins,
Your ends are spent,
The police are comin'
And your "friends" start runnin'…huh?

What profits a man to gain the world,
Lose his soul and can't stop the Hell
That's comin'????

(Chorus)

As I said, my life has been changed
Since Jesus is on the throne of my heart.
I took you within
Some of my inner, deepest parts
And here we stand at the crossroads.
I told you the path I choose.
Every day is not easy and it's narrow.
But by following Jesus, I can't lose.
But to go with the flow
Do what everybody else is doin',
I've done that before, I know.
The path is wider and much easier.
They both have eternal destinations
But choose wisely which way you will go.

Not In Control

Holy Spirit, siege my soul.
Take control.
As I grow old,
The more I realize
I'm not in control.

These Regrets

(Song)

(Chorus)
"I don't have time
To maintain these regrets
When I think about…
I don't have time
To maintain these regrets
When I think about…"

Letting go, letting go, letting go,
Of all the things I didn't know
Letting go, letting go, letting go,
Of the places I shouldn't go.
Letting you know,
Letting me know,
Letting us know
That it's okay to learn from our mistakes.
Letting you know

Letting me know
That it's okay to take the stage
And your heart still quakes.

(Poem)
It's a part of the human condition
It's a part of life
He gives us permission
To try and to get it right
He sets up conditions
Means for us to be forgiven
For being less than
Perfect, a way to be loved perfectly
Without it costing us anything.
Just our willingness to receive
His love…

(Chorus) 4x

Letting go, letting go, letting go,
Of all the shameful heartbreaks

Letting go, letting go, letting me know,

Of the all the ones who betrayed
Letting you know,
Letting me know
Letting me know
When you forgive your mistakes
Letting you know
Letting me know
Be the sender of grace
To the offender, anyway.

(Poem)
Trust Him with the outcome
That it's okay to give it to Him
Living a life of total surrender
He is the ultimate heart mender
He restores us back to norm
And can guide us through any storm
So if failure is impossible
What would you try anyway?
What big prayers would you pray
As your heart still quakes…

In His love…

(Chorus) 2x

"So we don't have time
To maintain these regrets
When we think about…
We don't have time
To maintain these regrets
When we think about…"

Power In My Pen

My power is in my pen.
Power in my tongue.
What I say.
What I communicate.
I build up
Or tear up.
So I won't give it up to you.
I've set fair boundaries for me,
To protect you.
Keep crossing them.
Keep pushing
And you may hear what you don't want to.
So, instead of giving you that satisfaction,
I take action and block, delete and repeat.
I'm grateful for choice.
Is it positivity or negativity?
Grateful for the ability to choose.
I can give my energy to mitigated speech
Or redirect it to endeavors more fruitful.

Shake the dust off my feet.
Take back my peace and keep on moving.
You can't say on Judgment Day
That you didn't know.
A prophet is without honor
In her own home.
So if He tells me to say it,
I'll try to use tact.
At the same time,
Some folk don't know how to act.
So hopefully this comes out right
And with love.
Everybody has a point where
They've had enough,
And must protect their souls.
I'd rather use this gift to speak
Heavenly decrees.
Manifesting what He wills on Earth
As it is in Heaven.
Speaking peace and love,
Uplifting the Brethren.
I'm not one for constant judgment
Or loving to give correction

Because it's a double-edged sword.
At the same time,
I'll be instant in season
And speak His Word.
So there's power in this pen.
There's power in my words.
I choose to outline my boundaries,
Possess my territories
And be slave to no man.
Or to man's opinion pimping
And distorting God's vision.
Setting order and reform
Doesn't make tight friends,
But can stir up enemies.
At the same time,
He's overcome the world,
Death, Hell and Pharisees,
So what can man do to me?

The Silent Intersection

Distinct hum
Motors roar
Wheels run
Interstate
On the porch late
Distant vehicles
Murmur...
My predilection

The Intersection
Street light
Sweet night
Peace night
Balmy
I write
While it's quiet
I write
Sitting tight

Feline
Perched quiet
Observant
Servant
Fervent
Emergent
Allergic to fear
Change is near
Listen...

One bird chirp
A new sound
Is birthed
Trembling
The earth
Giving all
It's worth
To assert
The Creator lives!

And He's present
Even when
It's silent.

Everything sensed
Feeling resident.
I'm home.
And He's at home
In me.
Shalom.

Mr. & Mrs. Pro Life

You say don't have an abortion, right?
I'll go to Hell if I don't choose life.
I'm not condoning murder.
I'm not co-signing sin.
I'm just asking questions
Just trying to see the justice
In your judgments.
Because having this baby
Is a commitment for life,
And I didn't see you supporting him
At the most important times
In his life.

So just pulling off the covers
Of blanket statements,
Many don't realize what they're saying,
Missing the opportunity
To be a true witness
As the Bible suggests.

So, I chose life.
Even dedicated him to your church
But where were you
When I had to work?
Were you there when I needed a ride
After just giving birth?
Were you there
When we needed a place to stay?
How many times did you help us move?
How about when he needed a mentor?
A male figure to show him God's way.
Not just on Sunday
Or youth trips
But going to his games
Like when you watched your sons play?
Where were you when he ran away?
You promised to check on him
On Saturdays.
You told a broken boy to call *you*
Then, never answered when he needed you.
So busy focused on feeding the children
Out there.

When missions for Christians
Is right here.
Every day.
Right next door.
Beyond a donation here and there.

So, tell me,
Are you doing anything
About the school to prison pipeline?
The one that preys upon the fatherless?
What are you doing daily
To prevent prison ministries?
Or to prevent our children from being
murdered
In the streets
By each other
And police brutality?

Where are you, Mr. & Mrs. Pro Life?
We only found a few
Along each station in my son's life
Who were willing to be there,
Be family

And pour into his life.
Twice when he was little,
Because I was a single mother
Christian parents
Told their sons not to date me.
But I chose life? Right?
Though Jesus carries their baggage daily,
Christian families chose to reject him
And me.
Of course, looking back,
Hindsight is 20/20.
And He worked it all for our good but
It could've been a great witness
Of Christ's redemptive love.
So dear Christians,
You owe God, you owe us
And our children
An apology.
You're saying one thing
But not committed to following through.
Saying what sounds good
But unwilling to pay the cost
To carry the cross

You lay on others
To shoulder by themselves,
Especially, if your sons
Are procreating the children
And paying for the abortions,
Dear Mr. & Mrs. Pro Life.

Audience of One

Wednesday, watched a man
Rally the city to fix a park and tennis courts.
Older, wealthier land owner, White male.
Reached out to the Mayor
And got immediate action.
The irony, that I've called the law,
Been to court,
Numerous times for help more sacred;
Protection of myself and my son,
Not receiving the same patronage
Or solution.
Instead, gaslighted, accusations,
Left to fend for myself.
I could be envious of this man
But I have an audience of One.

Not saying that he doesn't.
And favor isn't fair.
I drive what he drives,
I exercise

At the park where he parks
At retiree's time
Because I have an audience of One.
People are still trying to figure out
How I've got what I've got
Or have done what I've done.
I can't contribute it to anyone
But the Father, Spirit and Son.
I have an audience of One when I pray.
He is intent to my lips;
He hears every word I say.
I think a thought,
He hears it afar off.
He is so concerned about me.
I'm still trying to catch up
With the revelations of how
He feels about me.
Even in this life when it gets oppressive,
When it gets depressive,
Worries, obsessing,
People not getting me,
Little support, it gets real lonely.
But with Him, I don't have to fake it.

The more real I am with Him,
The more He helps me make it.
The compassion He gives me,
Teaching me how to love myself,
Giving me capacity to have compassion
For the ignorant who underestimate me
Based on the outward.

Lord, they don't know,
Don't realize the inner power
That comes from relationship with You.
You wired strength in my DNA.
So, it doesn't matter what they do or say.
So I stand, in the natural alone,
Holding Your hand in the Spirit,
Surrounded by angels, swords drawn.
Knowing when I give the command
Of Your Word, they'll hear it.
Because I have an audience of One.
Like Esther,
Taking counsel with the Father, Spirit and
Son.
Being rewarded for what's done, in secret.

Expectancy

To the Body:

Serving others is rough.
It's easy to take on
The mentality:

"I cut them off
Before they can cut me."
Been there before.
Love hurts deep.
But with You, Lord,
I wait...
In expectancy.

With my heart open
Vulnerable
To disappointment,
Vulnerable
To resentment,

Vulnerable
To contempt,
For no one is exempt
From rejection...

Eyes up,
Palms up,
Holes from where my flesh
Is put to death.

Dying daily
To the waiting,
To the comparing,
People staring
As I wait on my blessing.

Humph...
I knooooow my Daddy's
Coming for me!

Palms up,
Eyes up,
Expecting You to bless me

Indeed, and my seeds
Lord, enlarge my territory.

No, no honey...
Ishmael won't do.
Instant gratification
Verses the uncomfortable
Wait station?
I will stand on faith,
Looking up at the stars
I can't count.
Believing beyond doubt,
Isaac is about
To manifest.
Yes, God's best
The gift to propagate
The earth,
Redeeming creation with its birth.
This blessing
Isn't about you
Or me.
It's all for God's glory
So, we wait

In expectancy....

Daddy, You said,
"Behold You set before me
An open door!"

You said that new things
Are springing forth,
So let us see them!
Lord, open our eyes,
Make all things new!
Giving You permission
To remove what's
Obstructing our view!
Because Holy Spirit,
We've got WORK
To do,
And You've given us
ALL the tools!
So, Teacher,
Teach us what to do!

Guarding our hearts, yes,
For out of it flows
The issues of life.
But keep us warm
And sensitive,
Breaking off any ice
From our hearts.
Cuz Lord knoooows
It gets cold...
While we wait,
But Your heartbeat
Keeps us warm
As we anticipate.

In expectancy
Of what God
Promised you
And promised me.

Palms up,
Eyes up,
Expecting You to bless us
Indeed, and our seeds,

Lord, enlarge our territories.

Cuz we know

Our breakthroughs are coming...

While we wait

In expectancy…

Laugh Out Loud

Why do I laugh so loud?
Because I realize
I'm no longer under a cloud.

Why do I laugh so loud?
Because what was plaguing me
No longer holds me down.

I am FREE!

The mindset of religiosity,
Thinking that following Christ is so hard
Because there's something wrong with me
Has died.
The joy of the Lord IS my strength!
I have all that I need
Because of His faithfulness.
The blessings of the Jews
Is upon me, too.

And my Father supplies
In Jesus' name
For me, the same.

Depression and oppression
Are far from me.
No longer a victim but a victor
By His authority given to me.

I am FREE!

Giving permission to others
To walk away from legality
Into a free, loving relationship with
The One who died for me.

I am FREE!

Her Craft

It's a man's world they say.
Think like a man, act like a girl.
Why must we be so divided internally
to be successful financially?
I've found it isn't the way for me.

Being Ignored

Being known
It seems to be
The hardest thing to do.

When everyone is interested
But not interested in you.
What do you do?
Force your way through?

No, you bask in
The best of you.
You stick to what's true.

You rehearse,
You practice
What your Creator
Says about you!

That's all you can do...

And pray.
God,
What am I to learn from this today?

Try to not take it personally.
Trust that God
Will cause you to shine
When it's time
For His glory in you
To show through.

Father, forgive them
For they know not
What they do.
I'll rest and abide,
Continue to shine,
Not hide my light.
Enjoying
Fellowship with You.

You Can't Cancel Me!

You can't rep me and be toxic!
That's NOT who I am.
If you can't handle people
With grace,
Don't say you understand!

If you don't like what
I'm saying, come talk to me.
Cuz I assure you honey,
You CAN'T cancel me!

Your opinion is NOT
My problem!
I HAD 99 of them
And YOU CAN'T solve them!

You can delete,
Block and unplug,
But my beliefs

Will no longer be
Swept under the rug!

You can shut me out.
I'll go where I'm welcomed.
You can mute my mouth
But with signing,
They will feel me.
Place me in chains,
Stop blood from
Flowing through my veins
But time won't
Never, ever, ever
Let you forget me.

Like Abel's blood stains!
You can't cancel me...

My Creator
Designed my impact to remain!

Pain & Purpose

As a woman.
Entrepreneur.
Intrepid mother.
Woman of color.
Who loves to break the status quo
But fears the rejection.
Hates being misunderstood.
The pain of being a pioneer
Is not for the faint of heart.
Like the strongest
Of drink,
It'll put hair on your chest,
Yet,
It can be so intoxicating...

It's the aftermath
That hurts like Hell.
Hail you then nail you
That's what people do...
Where do martyrs

Get to rest when their bodies
Are covered in lashes
From whips not meant for them,
Lashes meant to scare the piss
Out of anyone
Who dares to traverse
A road less traveled?
Your friends reach
Out their hands covered in
Salt granules of jealousy,
Unaware of how it stings
Because they're not risking
Bleeding openly,
Being mocked publicly
And now privately, too.

Is there rest for the weary?
Ministering to upcoming generations
With spiked teeth
Gnashing with
"What about me?"
Piercing the elders'
Hands & feet.

Why does the devil spend
So much time trying to silence me?
Especially
After a great victory?
Perhaps a mortal
Misunderstanding
But supernaturally...
Over and over
It'll behoove me
To keep you around.

So, I lay it all down...
At the feet of Jesus,
As you told me to go
When there was
No room at the inn.
Not even for you
To just listen.
Sad, but true
And it gives me hope.
Praying to Jesus
In times like these
The only One who doesn't

Interrupt me.
He listens intently
As human souls
Battered,
Sorely, we vent to Him.

He listens
Without judgment.
Offers time-tested wisdom,
Comfort & care,
Empathy & compassion
Because He's already been there.
And showed how He cared
On Calvary back there.

He also shared honest
Perspectives on man
Throughout the Good Book.
So, pioneers may cry at times
But we are never shook.

Inspired after a little break-away, not break-up & Speak Now by Leslie Odom Jr.

Be Happy

Happy.
Accomplished.
Settled.
Completed projects
Satisfied.

That's what happy means to me...
No!

Content.
Rested.
Stable.
Protected.
At peace with the world and oneself.

That's what contentment means to me...
No!

Perfection.

All my ducks lined in a row.
Got it all together.
Expert.
Excellent.
Winning.
Conquering.
Never hurting.
Never losing.

That's what I thought happiness was to me.
But with more trophies,
Peace lessens,
Wanting to fold under the pressure
To fit all my greatness
On the cover of your magazine.

Yes! I'm Billy Jean!
I'll be the face behind the scarlet letter!
I'll be the evidence of
What goes on behind the scenes.
I am the skeleton in the closet.
And guess what?
Dry bones can live.

Dry bones can grow.
Dry bones, they do talk.
Dry bones, yes, they do walk
Right out from death to life
And become a garden of life.

Being a being.
Knowing your worth,
Even if it comes from
Under the dirt.
Now that's happy!

Ms. Under Stood

Hi, it's me,
the one from the hood.
The anomaly.
The misnomer.
The one you say
Thinks she's too good.

The unhireable
Because there's
Something about her...
Yeah, too hood.
Yes, that's me!
Nice to meet you.

I'm Ms. Under Stood.
No, I'm not married.
Too beautiful to be single,
But not phony enough
To mingle.

Yes, I'm powerful
Enough to lead.

But all you see
Is the person who
Can wipe fannies
Or be your child's mammy.
Or baby momma in today's
Vernacular.

No, apologies,
I'm the CEO.
I know…
Yes, I know about
Tax brackets.
Eating sunflower seeds
And Lemonheads,
Sitting on the porch
Of the corner store
In the ghetto.
Full of street hustle
Without being in the trap.

So, what do you call that?
What can you say of that?
Proper speaking
Street Queen
Worshipping the
King of all kings.
Just call me Ms. Under Stood.

Moving In Silence

Hip hop taught me.
I was raised
A suburban girl
In the streets.
They said, "Real killers move in silence."
Like a samurai, I,
Don't advocate violence.
So, I choose to keep you out my business.
I realized you won't get this.
You won't support this
And the best way to learn
Is to show you
Better than I can tell you.

It's no need in begging you to value
What you got to enjoy for free…

I gave away my power
To a machine, sucking energy.

My time,
My expertise,
My intellectual property,
It came so effortlessly
So, it seemed.
It costed me,
Not you.
Never acknowledging
What I've been through
To learn what I know.
But it was my fault
For not realizing
My true value.

So, now I'll show you
Better than I can tell you.
The last time you asked,
I told you what I planned to do,
And all my plans fell through.
Was it because of you?
I'm not sure,
But I watch who tolerates
And who celebrates.

How folks react when I'm up
And when I'm down.

I've learned that there are those
Who only love you
When you're on their level
Struggling, too.
And there's those who
Will push you to be your best you.
There's those who you must shut out
Because they direct you in the way
They are going instead of what's true to you.
And there's those who will block you
Or ignore you,
Hoping you'll shrivel and go away.
But they find out that
When God has appointed you,
You're here to stay.

I was never one
To keep friends close
And my enemies closer.
Too much energy watching my back.

So, I'll finish up these accomplishments
In secret.
And if I can afford to,
I'll pay attention to how you react.
You get a rise out of gossip.
I live for making an impact.

Challenger

It's who I am.
Settle?
No sir!
No, thank you ma'am!
I DARE you to reconsider some things!
I BET you won't change!
I'm sorry...did I just push you?
It's what I do!
Why? Because there's more in you!
And the world needs the BEST you!
Not the one you're settled to.
Don't let this sweet smile fool you.
Behind it, is a passion so powerful!
I'm in your life to CHALLENGE you!
MOVE or be MOVED!

Parenting & Protecting Legacy

A job that comes with no description,
yet is designed to be managed by two,
plus a village.
What do you do when
"the ideal"
doesn't happen to you?
Do your children blame you?

Confessions of An Independent Mother

Outside in the rain,
Putting air in my leaky tire again.
I hear the thought, *Why didn't you ask him?*
But I responded to it, they, them:

"See, I don't mind you helping me
But being a damsel in distress
Gets me in a big mess.
See service is my love language.
Since I've been left with
All this responsibility
Of raising men on my own,
Not being able to be a child,
Had to be grown,
You're helping me makes me feel like
Daddy's finally home.
And some of you know it.

Playing on the tune that chivalry is dead.
It's not,
But his daddy is.
So, you carry my groceries,
Have coffee,
We laugh,
Intently you listen,
Guard down now
'Til my panties are slippin'???

So, don't help me.
Don't pray for me
While You have sin
That's undealt with,
Then you prey upon me.
Just because my house looks empty
Doesn't mean my head is."

Just an independent mom's confessions...

"People Child's" Child

(Dedicated to my son, Koi
You changed my life and I'm so proud to know you.)

I remember never wanting
You to be anything like me
When you were in my womb.
I felt so low, I didn't see any good in me.
But you manifested.
You grew and played in the stores.
Your smile was so infectious.
Then I saw all the goodness in me
Shine through you.
I remember being in A.C. Moore
With my aunt.
You were 3.
You found a little boy,
And you 2 became instant buddies.

It didn't matter
That he was Indian
And you were Black.
You felt so comfortable,
You asked the man with the boy
If he was his grandpa
But the man was really his dad.
See…
Like me, we walk in friendly curiosity.

So, I knew Indians
Can tend to have children
Later in life
Like Norah Jones' dad.
But you were a kid
And oh, the joy you had!

So, I see a lot of me in you.
And I wouldn't be who I am today
If I said "yes" to abortion
Which I thought was the only way.
But you transformed my life
Like no medical degree could.

Though I regret my missteps,
As a parent,
When they told me I'd be a good one,
At 19, I couldn't imagine it.
A solitary family unit of 2.
I've always been so proud of you!
Even as a Nudie Butt
Dangling around the living room.

I love your patience
To turn foes to friends.
I rarely had the patience
But you forgave over & over again.

"A panther who gives mercy,"
That's what I named you
And, oh, how true!
A man of strength
With a humble stature towards God.
Anytime I started to teach about Him,
You'd naturally sit on the ground, intent,
Legs crossed.
In my womb, I always knew

There was something special about you.
It's part of why I'd fight for you.
I've sold all my furniture, quit jobs,
Just to provide and protect you.
Everything I've learned
About Christ, life, leadership, money,
business,
I've poured into you.
Because I knew
You would be great one day.
Placed you in circles
Where I couldn't go,
But was according to
The training up
In the way you should go.

Many times, I've gotten angry,
Crushed between a rock
And a hard place.
I was your first coach,
Ruling my house out of fear.
Saying things, I shouldn't say
Now wondering why you're not near,

But I hear.
I remember all the teaching,
All the affirmations,
Preachings,
All the blessings,
All the empowerment,
And prayers over your life
Over the years.
I'm praying over your children,
Praying over your wife.
And even now, I pray,
Over the challenges of life.
And as you'll see one day,
Kids don't come with instruction books,
But there's Google now,
And the ageless Good Book.

All the positive seeds
Planted in you will spring up
Upon each new challenge's arrival
Because you're chosen.
You've been set up not to survive,
But thrive and FLY!

You have always been.
You taught me without trying
The power I have within,
And
Your kids and life will teach you, too!
And with long life,
May God forever satisfy you!

Love,
Your Mika

Daddy's Girl

He is love.
I am loved.
I love
So deeply
Like dark green rivers
Full of mud
Tears on my shores
Being caressed
By coursing tenderness
By my breasts.
The same ones that give milk
Hardened in the cold
Says hello to gravity when I get old
And yes, I'm still loved.
I love deeply
Because I am His child.
I do what Daddy does.
El Shaddai,
Multi-breasted One.

He is love.
I am loved.
I love
So deeply.

He loves so deeply.
He designed lips
To kiss sweetly.
He loves so deeply.
The clouds sweep by,
Our eyes giving
Our skin rests from the sun.
A muse to draw
And make art,
A love so distantly near,
Giving us permission
To peer into the atmosphere
To the rest of His creation.
Giving us light in the dark
With stars
Like a loving Father,
Painting hearts on his daughter's

Room walls.
And hanging lights on her ceiling,
Giving her peace,
Knowing she has direction.
Never lost at sea
Because He holds the galaxies
In His hands for you & me.

Now, that's love…

The kind of love you build your world around
Like I built mine around you.
Devout loyalist,
Literally, my skin wrapped around your frame
Like a Picasso canvas.
A masterpiece was born
Yes, you.
Lovely you.
Smart you!
Adorable you!
Irreplaceable you!
In my arms for encouragement

And nourishment.
If I could wrap you in a midnight blanket
Full of tender stars,
I would
Because you light up my life
Like firewood,
The fuel to my desire
To protect and provide.
Just imagine how God feels
About me and you?
He loves so hard, too.
Giving an abundance of fresh air to breathe,
Multitudes of stars to see,
Bubbly outbursts of songs to sing,
Waves of oceans,
Forests of trees,
Birds and leaves,
Animals and creeping things,
Catering to our needs
Before we even asked.

So, if you wonder why my hugs
Feel like magic

Or my tears weigh a ton,
I am the daughter
Of the ultimate lover,
The Holy One
Who gave His only Son
To bring us back to Him.
The One who loved me right out of my sin.
He's my Dad.
And I'm just like Him.

He is love.
I am loved.
I love
So deeply.

Wise Mother

You're blessed when you meet Lady Wisdom,
when you make friends with Madame Insight.
She's worth far more than money in the bank;
her friendship is better than a big salary.
Her value exceeds all the trappings of wealth;
nothing you could wish for holds a candle to her.
With one hand she gives long life,
with the other she confers recognition.
Her manner is beautiful, her life wonderfully complete.
She's the very Tree of Life to those who embrace her.
Hold her tight—and be blessed!
With Lady Wisdom, God formed Earth;
with Madame Insight, he raised Heaven.
They knew when to signal rivers and springs to the surface,
and dew to descend from the night skies.

- Proverbs 3:13-20

A wise woman, a wise mother
Is more precious than rubies.
Priceless like diamonds of old.
Even if a rich man gave millions,

You are still worth more
Than your weight in gold!

A mother who is a part of the sheepfold of Christ
Has no price.
A praying mother plucks fruit from Heaven
With her words,
Piercing the heart of the enemy like a sword.
Declares her worth.
Her loving prayers
Protect the children she births.
Her wisdom multiplies
Treasures on Earth
To let you be first
Because she chose to be last.
She chose to sacrifice.
She decided to pray and fast.

Bless her with the honor due her.
Give fragrant flowers to her.
With honor and love,
She has labored well.

As she moves through the atmosphere,
She carries along peace.
Everyone looks to her for guidance.
As she parts her lips to speak.

Full of power
From sitting at His feet.
Her care runs wide.
Her love runs deep.
Pressing her children into His presence,
As she prays while they sleep.

It is my prayer
That the Lord continues to keep
All your lambs and sheep
None shall be lost!
All will submit to Christ
And take up their Cross.
Following Elohim.
May God grant you your desire
And manifest all your dreams!

Spotify On Random

Don't let the Holy Spirit be the DJ,
Spotify on random,
A radio station
I didn't pick.
Yolanda Adams comes on...
The years I couldn't cry
Burst
Wanting to change it,
Instead, I lean in.
How could I be a fool?
We went too fast.
We were in love.
Perfect for each other.
Crashed and burst into flames.

Young love.
It's just pain...
But it happened in front
Of my son.

In front of our church.
Devastation in despair.
Haunting memories
In a trunk of thoughts
I rummage through called,
"Where did I screw up with my kid?"
Scanning through the waste,
The remains,
The stench of yesterday...
Clue #1,002 why he hates you.
Why he's not speaking to me.
I screwed it up with another "daddy."
Destroyed his dreams...
After that, I REALLY thought,
I'd never be enough.
Let me go into supermom mode
A decade later and it's still not enough.
Parenting alone is rough!

God! How I tried to forget!
Bury my unworthiness,
Erase my regrets.
But this song is on,

Lying on the couch
On the cover
Has me in tears.
Wanting to redo the years,
But today I forgive myself
And receive the words
Of this song.
Fifteen years is too long
To carry pain.
I embrace all of me,
Even the mistakes.
I let my past go,
Trusting in love,
I'll win again.

Tidal Wave

I gave my all for him.
3 jobs.
Corns, bunions
Foot soaks because I worked doubles to feed
him when his daddy couldn't.
I cried.
I died again and again for him.
I laid bare with my loins open.
Shots in my back
For you to put shots in his back
With no apology.
No, *I'm sorry Ms.....*
Your son scared me
I watch too much TV
I watched too much COPS
I'm insecure in my manhood
Addicted to special ops games
And your son just happened to be
The target today.

The government has said
Time and time again,
It's just skeet shootin'
Keepin' our streets clean,
Ya know?
Exercising our rights,
OUR right to liberty.
It's the American way,
Right?
It's how DC's streets were paved
With blood.
Your sons'
Not mine,
And as long as it stays that way
We're fine...

But Sir, dear Mr. Serve & Protect,
You do not acknowledge
The milk sacrificed from my breasts.
Do you see us as human??
Or beasts???
All undetached thugs in the streets
You feel you need to keep clean?

Why is America & the world in an uproar,
Sir?
Here's what happened...
A tidal wave
The earth shook!
Mother nature said,
What the Fuuuu!!!
Yes, 2020 made Momma Earth CUSS!
She said...
Daddy God, IF YOU DON'T GET DEEZ CHILINS,
IMMA SHAKE SOME ITSH UP!!!!
Like Abel's blood cried from the earth.

He called his deceased Momma
To him, she gave birth.
And it evoked ALL of the Feminine energy!
It woke EVERY struggling Momma,
Worried if her child would return home safe.
It pissed off atmospheric presence!!!
We felt it in our wombs!
It caused volcanic explosions!
It caused tsunami floods.

It's not a video game, Sir.
Son, You spilled OUR son's blood.
Not just his family's tears broke.
You caused international streets to flood!
EEEEEEE-NOUGH!
IS ENOUGH!
If you want to fly your nation's flags proud again,
Make sure we ALL have justice!
Be ACCOUNTABLE
For EVERY nation's prejudices
And greedy, murderous sins.
EVEN profiting from low income
Families' abortions.

Again, our Moses', our Christs'
Assassinated by your Pharaohs & Herods
To keep your power so sacred...
Make sure ALL our children come home safely!
In the US and every corner of the earth,
If you want to pull that trigger,
If you want to kneel on another "nigger"

Remember the Womb-man,
The one who sheds blood to give birth.
She even did it for you...
Then and only then
Will your "Christian" values hold true.

More Than A Woman

I'm not like you.
You are not like me.
Comparison is the robber of peace.
All my life you've been programmed to look
outside yourself for contentment,
but it's time you give yourself loving
sentiments.
Here, I'll hold up the mirror for you,
Beautiful. ❤

The Mammogram

Take a deep breath.
Hold it. Squeeze.
Breathe. Release.

Take a deep breath.
Hold it. Squeeze.
Breathe. Release.

Sounds like the story of my life,
Minus the "breathe" part.
Well...short breaths
Here and there…
A gasp for more air
Because the overwhelm
Is about to come.
Boobs black & blue,
But I'm used to abuse;
It's good for you.
That's what they say, right?

He said, right?
She said, right?

So, take a deep breath.
Hold it. Squeeze.
Breathe. Release.

Take deep breaths
As often as you can
Because you don't know
When release season
Is coming,
If ever…
It's breathe now
Or never
In this fight
Of our lives
To protect
Our boobies,
Our bodies,
Our gifts
To nourish
To excite

To comfort
And uplift.
Beauty with profound purpose…
That's right…

So, take a deep breath.
Hold it.
Life will squeeze
But you're made for this.
You control the release.
You have the peace
And the power
Because you showed up for yourself!
You showed up
And enjoy the wealth
Of your healthy love of self!
Now breathe!
And release.
Everything that robs you of peace!
Every limiting belief
That says you should
Look or be shaped like another!
Every lie that says your time has past

And death is around the corner.
Let go of the fear!
Let go of the pain!
The trials were only for your sharpening
To increase your value!
Like a diamond under pressure
Or gold under fire,
You've heated well!
Show off your scars
Your value just went higher!
Now, take a deep breath!
And release!
Fall into peace…
Now you see what you're made of!
Beautiful, powerful
And **always** worthy of love!

Not Cinderella

I thought love was provincial,
But that's not who I am.
The demure
And silent type
That's not
I'm loud.
I'm boisterous.
I'm happy.
I'm free.
Are you?

I was taught
He had the biggest castle,
But I see he's just a man
Doing the best he can.
I thought he would
Slay all my giants
But that's unrealistic
Expectations.

Who wrote all these fairy tales,
Full of an old man's exaggerations?
And we wondered why it wouldn't work…
We're all expected, after children,
To have an ant-sized waist,
Always catering to your tastes
As you won every race
But never had time for me.
Not the beauty,
Not the babe,
But your best friend
For whom you said
The home was made,
But it, for them.
To prove you finely fit in
Yes, your friends
Who you never forgot to
Check in with.

I'm not the Cinderella type,
Pining in a tower,
Waiting for you to save.
I'd help you fight the giant.

I'm the one who freed the slaves.
And you shouldn't mind
But they lied to you, too.
Telling you,
Just play!
GI Joe's and video games,
Cars and trucks;
You mess up
And the woman is supposed to
Clean it up.
Not kitchen sets and dolls
For you,
You don't need to prepare for marriage.
What do you look like
Pushing a baby carriage?
Toughness and money
Will solve everything.
It's ok if you sow your wild oats.
Let a man do his thing.

And then we marry
And I have to raise you,
But I can't tell you nothing

Or you'll do the opposite.
Or grudgingly appease
Until I'm not looking.
This system is broken.
But we can find our own way.
Staying committed to love
And respect like we did
On the first date.
Read some books.
Get counseling.
Momma didn't buy the puppy,
But we grown now.
You bought milk
And the cow.
And just for that,
We'll work it through
To be an example
Of how one
Comes from two.

All of Me Loves All of Me

Who is she?
Waiting for applause,
Waiting for acceptance
From a dad long gone?
She is the girl
Who rarely enjoyed
The gift of shopping trips
With her mom
Or sisters.
Turned down by many misters
And she did a lot of
Heartbreaking, too.

She is not tall enough to model.
Body not shaped
Like a coke bottle.
But this same girl produced

A gentle, wise warrior.
A soldier, a son,
Without an epidural!
Yup, no pain medication
Until after he was born!

This body has sojourned
Up and down the east coast,
Canada to the Caribbean,
For work as west as Mississippi,
Because that's all she's had
Time and opportunity to see
As a single mom.
But blessed to grow up on shrimp
Seafood, burgers & cod.

She's capable of gaining weight,
Breastfeeding for 21 months
And losing 10's of pounds.
She's a walking miracle!
She's learning to love her body
Because she's so faithful to herself.
Not just for her aesthetics

Or mechanics
But she's also saucy, tight & ripe!
Putting grown men to sleep at night!
Boy! And can she cook?!
ANNND bake!
So, I love her
Like a fat girl loves cake!

I remember when my son was born,
At 19, so conscious of her fat,
Finding purpose while nursing,
He squeezed her back fat.
He found comfort and protection
In her presence,
In her essence.
The things magazines photoshop.
As a woman, friend, auntie to many,
Kids used to call her Auntie Squishy,
Because of the softness of her hugs.
Her fat wraps children in love.

But…
Movies don't teach us this.

TV shows say there's something wrong
With us and our breasts.
But she's learning to embrace herself.
Love herself from the inside out!
And did I tell you about her mind????

Yes, she's the one, instead of selling
Her food stamps for cash,
Which is common,
She decided to create,
Using her street knowledge,
Though she didn't finish college,
And sold sandwiches and cakes!
Wisdom is within her,
Though life tried to break her.
Did you know?
She used to break up fights
At 9, with her parents?
Sitting on her drunk stepdad's lap
As the mediator?
She set up meetings at 17,
To speak to her mother's pastors
About the way they preached.

About people being tardy
Which her mom took super personally
Because of her state mentally.
So, she's a girl of fire!
She's a rose in the concrete!
Though it took her until 40
To realize,
She needed to teach people
How to treat
Me.

Because all of her
Loves all of me.
All the hurts and imperfections,
All my boisterous laughing
And depression.
And the only way
I'll give my all to you
Is if you truly see my value
And not exploit me for what I can do
For you.
'Cuz I am finally starting
To accept and love all of me!

With Fire in My Hair

With fire in my hair
And snow at my feet,
I have the power to encourage
Or discourage and make weak.
In season, when I step,
I leave flowers in my wake
With healing in my hands
And His love upon my face.

My style ebbs and flows like the sea.
I cannot be placed in a box
So, get off of me.
God has enlarged my territory
A child of God is the only label for me.

Revolutionary is the magnitude
Of my anointing.
Like the clashing cultures
Of culminating cities.

From New York to D.C.,
Atlanta and Miami,
Chicago and Detroit,
Hollywood and L.A.,
Colorful and contrasting
Like electric blue and slate gray.
Turning the world upside down
Like when Jesus walked
The earth back in da day.

The apple didn't fall far from the tree.
When you see Him, you see me.
Revolutionary, rebelling against conformity.
Casting out the traditions of man
That clutter spiritual clarity.
And confuses who you are hearing,
Hoarding the blessings and not sharing;
Binding up silly women into yokes
Pilfering the poor and misleading folks.
So, I come and turn over tables,
Exposing weak doctrine as fables.
Taking it back like Anne of Green Gables.
Preaching, "Stop relying on man

And know that God is Able.
Open your bibles and turn off the cable!!!"

Being all things to all man
From CT to Japan
India, Buenos Aires, Jamaica
And from foreign to familiar lands.
Whether it's in Sioux Indian,
Blackfoot or Cherokee,
It doesn't matter
As long as the bread is fresh,
Serving Christ Jesus on a platter.

With fire in my hair
And snow at my feet,
I blow like the wind
And like His Word, I repeat!
Know that God is Able
Open your bibles and take off the labels!
It's not about who I am
Or what I look like,
It's all about Him.
Time is too short, so get right.

With fire in my hair
And snow at my feet,
Everywhere I go,
Signs and wonders follow me.
I leave flowers in my wake,
Every ordered step that I take
As His glory shines upon my face.

With fire in my hair
And snow at my feet,
He that have an ear
Let him hear.
The Lord is near,
To him that calls
Upon His name.
Come try Jesus, the real Jesus
Not the one they made up
And like me,
You'll never….

Be the same…

Gold Digger

You called me a gold digger,
Someone wanting something for free.
You called me lazy
When I'm one of the hardest
Women working.
So how could this be?
When saved or not,
Authenticity
Always gave me peace.
I don't do fake friends for fame.
So why would I
Bounce on your shriveled thing
When I've earned almost
Everything I've owned?
Nothing just given to me,
Not even when I had a need.
Being real makes my heart beat.
So how could I pretend
To like you, never mind love you

For a ring???
Maybe what you're saying
Is a projection of you on me,
And you're looking for a Sugar Momma
Because you're not mature enough,
And pockets ain't like God's.
So, you can't afford
To be my Sugar Daddy.

I Decided

I decided after Covid,
What if life ends?
Am I satisfied with my life?
After being Rapunzel
In a tall tower of religiosity,
"Let down your hair,
Make a list and long prayers"
They told me,
"And Boaz would appear."
I've been waiting here
For years and years.
Suitors walk on by
Then I realized
As long as I've tried,
They lied.
My type of hair doesn't grow that long.
So, there's a disconnect.
And here I was breaking my neck…
Grand momma said that
If I try, I'll break my neck,

But I already did.
So, let me try to see if I can fly.
So, I fell...

It was a short fall.
Now instead of holding my breath,
I exhaled though...
Landed no cradle at all,
But I'm standing flat footed
Ready for the world,
Ready for the game so I thought...
I decided

I wanted more in life.
So, I decided to lay
Legs up
As he pulled my dress up,
Off
And he filled my cup.
I decided to enjoy a life.
I longed for all those years in that tower,
Feeling the power of humanity
Inside me,

Even if it didn't last.
I decided to have
My spice,
My slice,
My bite of the American Dream,
For once.

I decided.
Now there's this life
Growing inside me.
Ignoring anxieties
That I'm birthing him
Into a life of dysfunctionality.
Relinquishing the fear of stares
Because I'm not 19 anymore.
Unsure of how his father will be
But I decided to open these doors
Knowing there's more for me.
So, I'm excited
About what God has in store.
Now let's see how supportive
The Church will be
Now that I've chosen pro-life…

Hopefully they won't condone
His or her life
To grow up on its own
Or be an adult police target.
I chose pro-life, right?
Yes, I decided.

At least I tried.
And I did fly.
Wings a little broken,
But I'm not imprisoned anymore.
I'm ok with me more than ever before.
That's what life is worth living for!

I decided.

The Jukebox

If I turn back time,
Rewind.
Replay all the songs I grew up listening to,
What did they tell me about love?
Cuz' haven't seen it before,
Not at my house.

So, I put some money in the jukebox
And heard "B**'s ain't sh*
But hoes n tricks..."
I realized that's not it,
But I loved it
Growing up.
As I developed,
It became my opposing,
Imposing, decomposing persona.
Wait, what's next on the list?
I need another hit.

Lauren Hill...

"Not wanting to be a foolish man's wife…"

"I just wanna be with you...

Nothing else I'd rather do…"

Mary J. "My Life"

The soundtrack of my teen years.

Well, dang! Were they there?

When God told Eve

Her desire would be for her husband…

God, we're in grace now.

Why is this curse

Still haunting me?

When did the chase reverse?

Royal Greatness

We all want to be loved.
It's our natural human need
But I can't see the bounds
Binding me.
Why him?
Why her?
Why not me?

A song that echoes
In the corridors
Of my soul,
Resonating to my thoughts,
Reverberating out of my body
Like rodent
Repellent.
Do they smell it?
'Cuz when they see me,
They say they see beauty
And body of course.

Built like a horse.
They ride me
But leave me in the barn.
Classic like something
Driven foreign
But not fit for the house?
Oh, just the couch?
You know...
Netflix n' chill.
If I will...

But I won't.
I have enough sense
Now to know
As far as you will let him
Is as far as he will go.

Oh!
But to be loved
For who I am,
Not just what I can do,
Makes putting myself
Out here

Being transparent
Worth it to find you.

Yes, you...
The one that comprehends
Feminine power
Not as a threat
But understands that leaving me free to be me
Is for your benefit.
That the prowess I carry
Comes with a disclaimer:
When you make the commitment
To marry,
There's no need
To try to tame her.
It's ALL yours...
The confidence,
The boldness,
The praise of her fans,
The blessing of her hands,
The anointing on her lips,
The rhythm in her hips,
Her stewardship

To make a dollar
Out of 15 cents,
It's ALL yours.
One flesh.
So, you are mine
And I, your Royal Greatness.

Binary Non-Binary Person

I'm writing this for conversation.
Hopefully, to have this one day with you.
With us, they, them, her, and him.
Why?
Because I feel we need to talk
And internet scrolling
And trolling won't do.

I want to get to know you
And at the same time,
Can you promise to try to hear me?
We both know struggles.
We both know hurdles,
Discrimination and hostility,
Yes, but I'm feeling misunderstood by you.
Your community.

Can we talk?
I'll tell you how.
Just a little background…
My grandma used to fuss at me
For always wearing men's jeans.
I was tall.
Women's jeans were too short.
She criticized me for wanting Hot Wheels
Some days,
With the matching car wash
Instead of Barbies
From Bradlees,
Though Barbies
And dolls I had plenty.
I played in the mud.
I helped my granddad
Uproot stumps.
I drive faster and better
Than many men.
I dreamed of being the next
Mark Martin.
As a teen, High Tech boots
And a Carhart jacket

Are what I wanted.
And Grandma bought it
From Jimmy's Army and Navy.
Refused to wear a purse
'Til 16.
And still do, mostly.
It's pockets **all day** for me!

I still like stuntin'!
Glad I had my son.
Without him to calm me down,
I always said I'd hurt myself
On a motorcycle
Wheelieing down Route 1.
So, was I non-binary growing up?
Perhaps.
But I learned to embrace
Who I am.
And I love all people
For being people,
And we all deserve justice and peace.

As a Black woman,

Single mother,
I worked for a bank in 2005,
When Connecticut first accepted
Civil unions.
I struggled to pay health benefits
As one individual with one dependent.
But two income earners in one house,
If they had a spouse or partner,
Paid less than me providing for my son.
I saw where people wanted to compare
The struggles of Pride and gay rights
With that of Martin Luther King's,
But I still grappled with how many options
The Pride community has in places like
The Big Screen,
Entertainment and acting.
How many Oscars does
Your community have
Compared to ours?
Can I walk into a job or store
And at face value…?
No pun intended.
I recall cases like

When the Supreme Court
Ruled in 2020
Against discrimination in the work place,
The victory for other groups of color
That won that week also
Were temporary,
Not permanent like in your case.
So, I wonder sometimes,
Does your community have better lawyers?
More money?
More power?
More access?
Or the option to be judged or not
Simply by choices in dress?
I'm being honest.
Please share with me intelligently.

I'd like to have these open honest
conversations
Without soundbites of my words being
picked apart.
I'm the same girl who spent time
In the Rainbow Center, at UCONN,

To ensure my gay friend
Wasn't bullied and felt safe from harm.
I sat in support groups and wore my
Ally button
Proudly.
So, when did things change all of a sudden?

I'd say also, since 2020,
I've had to fight harder to breathe.
Not just as a Black person,
But also, as a Christian.
In women's empowerment groups,
I would be chastised and criticized
If I didn't say things right.
But weren't these women the same people
Shutting down the "Karens"
And marching on my Black behalf?
But now my faith must be silenced
Because of another person's
Abuse of religion and misrepresentation of
Jesus?
Isn't the first amendment about freedom of
speech

And religious rights?
So we can each be who we are made to be?
I won't disrespect you by not agreeing.

This may seem controversial to some,
But I need time to adjust.
I need time to embrace thousands of new
normals.
That doesn't mean I don't like you.
That means that what I used to hold true
May not be what settles well with you.
And that's okay.

I'm open to understanding
But I've also experienced
A lot of hate.
And folks who still want me to be an ally
But don't understand how
"Proud Boys. Stand down. Stand back."
And the insurrection
Jeopardized my life.
And how I think about children
And their futures and the decisions

We are making now.
Doesn't mean that I judge adults
For their private lives.
At the same time,
If my child were still in school,
I'd have a lot to say about sex ed
And the curriculum.
To me, what and how my children are taught,
That's very personal.
So please, respect me for that.
And if you're judging me
And don't have children,
I forgive you for that.

Just like in the political system,
Like in creation,
There *should* be room for gray and color.
Not just Black and White,
But a plethora of shades.
How they all come together,
I don't know…
To be honest,
All I'm asking you

And your community to do,
Is hold space for my uncertainties
As a person,
Whether non-binary or binary.

Peace. Piece.

Peace. The piece.
Piece be still.
Give my soul time to heal.
Didn't have time to feel.
Watching the thief
Steal, destroy and kill.
One by one by one,
Dreams shattered.
Stepped over like glass
That didn't matter.
Things blew over like grass
But left night terrors
Of gun blasts
That night when the last dream
Was martyred.
Murdered actually.
I remember the event exactly.
It was 1989
If I recall correctly,

When life changed so
Silently, yet dramatically.

After that, I had a license to kill
Before I could drive.
It would be the last time,
If I could help it.
These dream thieves
Couldn't get me,
So I thought...
So, I waited
On the porch of my heart
Long, long, long after dark.
Weapon in hand and ready,
Just in case my innocence
Came under attack again.
It did.
But my weapon jammed.
So, I crammed all the tears
In my socks to cry later.
The milk was already spilt,
Packed my knapsack with guilt
And moved away.

Maybe they won't find me here.

I finally relaxed
For the first time in years.
It started to feel like home.
Fresh air, no cares,
Peace of mind,
No fights,
Restful sleep at night.
'Til one night it happened, again.
This time by a friend
I thought I could share
The love of stars with.
After that, because we were friends,
I was in the stolen vehicle
As the accomplice,
Though it was my goods that were
Taken, again.

So, it must be me.
Maybe this is the way it's supposed to be.
Comply and no one gets hurt.
Like a bank heist,

Cops sleeping on the job.
Don't know if I should be mad at them.
Because they were there, unlike my Pops.

'Til this day,
I take the gun.
I hold it to my head
And get in the bed.
I wait for the trigger to pull
Like my pants.
Every time I lie,
I die from the inside,
Wishing my innocence was ransomed
From this Groundhog Day,
Deja vu,
And though…

Christ,
I've given my life to You,
Every so often
A body snatcher will come
Like a sheep dumb.
I fall to the venom that

Makes me numb,
Expecting a different outcome,
Hoping to find value in myself.

Jesus, I really want love and intimacy.
Someone to love me for me
And not just want my body.
Someone to take the time to know me.
Someone I can trust to do what's best for us,
Not just go after what he lusts.
Someone who gives and not just takes.
Lord, help end this cycle of...

Despising the Scarlet Letter

Your accent is like a
Sweet fragrance to my ears,
Like roses to my nose.
Your sensitivity brings me to tears.
In your presence, it's hard
To stay composed.
I want to run away;
I feel foreboding joy.
Will this feeling go away?
Because I want more.

It's not fair!
It's not Spring,
But yes, love is in the air.
Is this Pandora's box
Or perfumes of thanksgiving
From broken alabaster?

A year's worth of making a living?
Whatever it is,
I keep singing
From the joy of meeting you,
From connecting with a heart
Like yours.
Innocent baby boy eyes.
Beautiful, inside and outward.
A humble intellectual.
Masculine protector.
Your care of me
Feels so foreign.
Are you my Xerxes?
Hold out your scepter.
This luxury is what
I should be used to
And I will get used to,
Realizing this is what I deserve
As your Esther.

Conflicting emotions of anxiety
And bliss.
I'm trying to lean into this

Without losing it.
Pictures of perfection and piety
In my head;
I fit none.
Men flock from outside the church
But inside,
Bow your head,
Close your eyes…
Is there a one?
Is there one…
Is there one…?

And when there is,
Is he an angel clothed in light?
We've all experienced that type.
So, a single, saved, sexy sister
Like myself
Has struggles in this isolation
Because single church men
If you can find them,
May flirt a little and that's ok.
Yet, they don't pursue.
They don't chase.

But these men in the world
Don't play no games.
They go after what they want
And it tends to be
Daughters of Zion.
And we know they can be
Wolves in sheep's clothing.
And at the same time,
We keep trying and trying
To stave off recurring cycles
From our past and ancestors' decisions,
Staying holy and chaste
Within the world with a touch
Of man's traditions.
So, we're waiting and waiting,
Waiting for Boaz, Jacob, James or John.
Flockin'.
Tons and tons of Ishmaels
Jockin'.
Cains ain't able,
But Cyrus' and Billy Bobs
Keep askin', seekin' and knockin'.
But no godly men are signing up

For the job, forget the date.
So, we sit, we sanctify and isolate
In secret shame,
Removing soul tie after soul tie
After soul tie, so we think.
Buying more makeup,
Getting more degrees
Because quiet as it's kept,
There's shame whispering,
"What's wrong with me?"
When really, not much,
It's just the world we live in.
We're trying to fight off desire
While fitting into a Eurocentric
Form of being a Christian,
While taking batteries out of
Biological clocks
While many men of color
Are in a cell block.
Justly or unjust
Or what about the drug game,
That since the 70's,
The Black community

And our families
Have never been the same?
The burning of Rosewood
To the bombing of North Tulsa,
It's been difficult to be united
In these states of America.
But like the Footprints
Poem in my mom's living area,
Black single mom and grand mom,
Jesus keeps carrying ya'.

There's nothing wrong with you
Or me.
We just are.
He just is
A God of justice
And it just is…
Going to change
And work out for our good
From the suburbs to the hood.
Let Your kingdom come,
Your will be done
On Earth as it is in Heaven.

And all that the enemy
Has stolen and enslaved
Be restored seven
Times seventy
To me and my community.
This is the season for restoration.
The flowers are blooming
And reblooming at and before
Their time.
I am worthy of good godly love.
To desire it, I will not be ashamed,
And I will accept nothing less.
And Saints, dear church folk,
If I bring a "heathen" to church,
Y'all better pray
For him to get saved
Instead of talking about me.
And pray if he's a Rahab
Or a Ruth
That these Christian men in this piece
Will be just as godly.
Because it's unfortunate
When we find more faithfulness

In Gentiles than Jews...
That's why God looks at the heart
And doesn't go by your views.
Married saints, I ask of you:
If you see singles,
Support them like never before.
Your shepherding will stave off wolves
But if you're only mindful
Of "us four and no more,"
Or who's after your mate,
You're missing your blessing.
The Scarlet Letter belongs
On your chest, not mine.
Aren't you Christ's bride?
But you're creeping
With the pride of life.
Many married believers
Know the blessing of
Being a mentor to our kids.
Wasn't God adamant
About the widow and the fatherless?
Isn't that what makes our religion undefiled?

In their distress, see about someone else's
child?
Single parent or widow or widower,
Today it's the same thing.
And that is another poem
In and of itself
That would solve many of the
Problems we see today.

So, in spite of it all,
I've learned to say,
I've learned to pray;
Seek what He says about me,
Not my single state.
Knowing that my purpose
Isn't just wrapped up in
We cutting the wedding cake.
Dear Jesus,
Your Hebrew accent is like a
Sweet fragrance to my ears,
Like roses to my nose.
Your sensitivity brings me to tears.
In Your presence, it's hard

To stay composed.
I want to run!
I feel foreboding joy.
You desire the best for me
And I happily despise the shame.
Joyfully I receive Your blessings!
Your Word says that
You're committed to me
And my seed.
And no matter if humans
Understand or can see
Or act justly,
As the word *righteousness* means
In Hebrew and Greek,
You are my strong tower,
Protector and provider,
And You will never leave!
Continue to keep me in Your company!

Amen.

To Granny

Beautiful one,
The Lord has need of you!
The best is yet to come!
You have a great work to do!

Your prayers have power.
Your praise shakes the earth.
Eye has not seen.
Ear has not heard.
The world cannot contain
What you are about to birth!

I Am Wanted

I am wanted.
Not just needed.
Not just tolerated.
But wanted.

I am wanted.
Not just for what I can do,
But for who I am.
I am wanted.

I am wanted.
Desired, beloved, cherished,
Adored and honored.
I am wanted.

I am wanted.
Celebrated,
Not just tolerated.
I am wanted.

If I never do another good deed;
If I never say the perfect thing;
If my beauty is marred;
My body disfigured
Like a shredded $100 bill,
My soul still
Holds its value.

I am wanted.
I will say this to myself
Until everything around me
Matches this poem,
This declaration,
This prayer.
And anyone or anything
That is opposite of it
Will no longer be there
Because I am wanted.

I Will Be Heard

Poignant
Polished
Presentable
Powerful
I will be heard.

Pleasant
Pious
Prosperous
Peasant
I will be heard.

Soliloquy
Monologue
Va Jay Jay
Feminine
Prose
I will be heard.

Poetry

Song

Dance

Write

Take flight

No fright

I **will** be heard.

Another Ms. Under Stood

Story Time!

Elkanah had two wives, Hannah and Peninnah. Peninnah had children, but Hannah did not. On the days Elkanah presented his sacrifice, he would give portions of the meat to Peninnah and each of her children. And though he loved Hannah, he would give her only one choice portion because the Lord had given her no children. So Peninnah would taunt Hannah and make fun of her because the Lord had kept her from having children. Year after year it was the same—Peninnah would taunt Hannah as they went to the Tabernacle. Each time, Hannah would be reduced to tears and would not even eat. "Why are you crying, Hannah?" Elkanah would ask. "Why aren't you eating? Why be downhearted just because you have no children? You have me—isn't that better than having ten sons?" Once after a sacrificial meal at Shiloh, Hannah got up and went to pray. Eli the priest was sitting at his customary place beside the entrance of the Tabernacle. Hannah was in deep anguish, crying bitterly as she prayed to the Lord. And she made this vow: "O Lord of Heaven's Armies, if you will look upon my sorrow and answer my prayer and give me a son, then I will give him back to you. He will be yours for his entire lifetime, and as a sign that he has been dedicated to the Lord, his hair will never be cut." As she was praying to the Lord, Eli watched her. Seeing her lips moving but hearing no sound, he thought she had been drinking. "Must you come here drunk?" he demanded. "Throw away your wine!" "Oh no, sir!" she replied. "I haven't been drinking wine or anything stronger. But I am very discouraged, and I was pouring out my heart to the Lord. Don't think I am a wicked woman! For I have been praying out of great anguish and sorrow." "In that case," Eli said, "go in peace! May the God of Israel grant the request you have asked of him." "Oh, thank you, sir!" she exclaimed. Then she went back and began to eat again, and she was no longer sad.

- 1 Samuel 1:2, 4-18□□

Despair is in the air.
Feeling
Isolated
On the lower end
Of the priority list.
Trying to make a dollar
Out of 15 cents.
Like Hannah,
Pouring out your soul
They answer as if

You don't make sense.

So what do you do?
You curl up inside of you,
Safest place to be?
Possibly not
But it feels a lot safer
Than the risk of being
Misunderstood, again.

My hormones were off kilter
Because of birth control.
Cycles unpredictable.
Laughing one minute,
Mad the next.
Crying the other
In my home alone.

In a calm moment,
On the phone,
I was trying to count my blessings.
I said, *I have so much to be thankful for…*
They said, *You sure do!*

Want me to tell you
the first?
I said, *Sure...* though in mid thought...
You woke up this morning. That's the first thing
to be thankful for! You woke up.
And I said, *And if I didn't, that wouldn't be so*
bad either.
They kept talking...trying to assure and
console.
Quietly I listened
As I tend to,
Regardless of the anguish in my soul.
Yet, people keep talking
When listening.
Creating an emotionally safe space
Is what heals.

I wasn't saying, and don't want to be suicidal
But my point was, you didn't let me finish.
And secondly,
You don't seem to be aware
Of my family dynamics.
The dysfunction and diaspora.

Many of which are in Heaven.
Jesus, mom, dad, grandparents,
Siblings and a baby,
And I plan to go.
So, no, I don't plan to stop my soul.
But in these last 2 years
The comfort isn't here.
It is written, *It's not good for man to be alone.*
So, thankfully the Lord knows
The anguish of my lonely,
Isolated soul.

Desperate for community,
Someone who understands me.
The ones who belong to me,
Year after year,
Holiday after holiday,
Whether my days are sunny
Or grey.
So, is that you?
Possibly not
If you're not listening.
Silencing what makes you uncomfortable

When the human need
Is to know you
And to be known.
In - to - me - see.
Intimacy.
Empathy & listening
Will meet that need in community.

So let's slow down
Ask questions
Don't be quick to throw clichés.
Who knows whose life
You might save?

The Wanting

I really, really, really
Wish you could understand
The anguish of the soul
When a woman can't give birth.
Those women who are wanting,
Those women who are longing
To bring life to the earth.

It's a painful torture
Every time our cycles come.
Is there one?
Is there some?
Is there the ability
To be what my body
Was created to be?
And it's acting like it,
But there's nothing
But intense shame.
What's wrong with me?

Why not me?

To be Mommy
And you Daddy.
Giving life to children,
Nurturing faces
That look like you and me.
Women, we get
To the point we don't care
If we suffer,
Bleed
Near to death
Or struggle financially.
We stab needles in our thighs
To give life!

Oh, it's a painful thing.
And it makes you crazy.
I'm in my 30's,
I'm in my 40's,
I'm in my 50's,
I'm in my.....
My body is aging,

Changing,
Yet, I still want a baby!
It hurts going to the parks,
Seeing parents with their kids,
Reminding myself of the tantrums
And the teenage rebellion
Or feeling like a failure
When your marriage
Falls apart in front of them,
Just to take my mind off the longing.
A sense of belonging,
A family again…

But this desire is so strong,
I'd almost subconsciously
Destroy the love we make.
Throw out the baby with the bath water.
This way,
I won't spend another month sobbing.
That we make all this love
And there's nothing
To show for it.
Nothing to comfort

This empty promise,
This emptiness,
This empty nest.
And you're not here
Or you can't understand
Or comfort these tears,
Flowing down my breast
In irony.

Like the story of Hannah,
I know you love me,
But it's not about you.
The burden of society
And child-giving
Can be so overwhelming
For me,
Crushing beneath the desire
To hold my own baby.

Even adopt
But where's my hubby?
I don't want to hear another prophecy
Or Bible story,

Especially if I'm still single
And Boaz hasn't appeared to me.
A woman
Who's barren.
Yet, pregnant with promise.
Full of doubts like Thomas,
Looking to God, being honest.
Lord, deliver me!

Outsider

Don't lead me on…
It's not what
I'm wanting you to do…
If you weighed a soul,
What would be its value?

God, it's not good
For man, humans to be alone,
You say.
I've had spiritual people tell me
The moat around my soul
Is my fault.
I need to get closer to You, more.
More, time with You, Lord
But to be honest…
That has cost me so much.
Marriage, children,
My family tree...
They say You give and take

They didn't say You'd take everything.
Everyone.
Even my son
Is far away.

Blame.
I can't admit I blame You.
But I don't know how to
Get this shame removed.
So I've been "working on me".
Running from You.
And ignoring things,
Not listening
To the voices
That there's something
Wrong with me.
Boundaries,
Therapy,
Tapping,
Praying,
Tearing down walls,
Intentionally reconnecting,
Trying to fight this forcefield

That keeps love away.

Why won't love stay?
What's it like to be supported
And around people who truly love me
And aren't going anywhere?
Trustworthy.
Who know me,
We have history.
I mean ***my*** people
My flesh and blood,
Or those who would fight for me,
Give to me,
There for me always
Like I'm their flesh and blood,
A son.
Being an orphan young
Empty holidays
For decades.
No set place to go home to
Begins to wear on you.
While you watch others
Take for granted

What you long to be invited to.
As the Church gets divided
By politics,
Losing its value
Of authentic love and community.

So I sit alone, questioning…
Is it the anger?
Because I've seen worse.
Is it my gender
My color
My community
Lord, is it a curse?
The anger
The depression
It's the pain
Of a tender heart
Left out
In the rain
Fending off the wolves
By herself.
The outsider
People pleasing

Moving around to build
A patchwork of community
The one who's loved by so many
But belongs to nobody.

What's that feel like?
Promises of being a bride…
When everyone loves you
Only from the outside.
When they value what you can do
But can't see your soul's value.
Or you're a trinket taken off the shelf
Enjoyed for himself
But won't share you with his family
Or anyone else…

Marriage of Approval

If he loves me,
Will you then receive me?
Will you see me
When it's "us"
And not just "me"
And my child?

I can say like Suge Avery
"I say isa married now!"
Running after clergy,
Waving a chip on my finger,
Hoping you'll finally
Acknowledge me,
Redefine my life
As a whole.
Not a struggle.
Not a part.
Not a charity case,
But a woman of God

Who can be approached
Without your jealous wife?

This need for "daddy's" approval
Led me to shattered
Dream after dream.
Into the ministry
Of codependency.
If you accept my anointing,
Promote me as a minister
Of more than children's church
Or outreach.

It's ok though...
I'm not waiting for Boaz
To rescue me anymore.
Your opinion of me
Isn't my fault.
I'm STILL going to answer God's call.
Hence, this book of art.
The process was necessary.
Maturity was definitely needed.
Marriage will be

Because I actually approve of myself,
Not what others think of me.
I'll actually be happy.

I now know approval
Starts within me.
Embracing
If God be for me,
Who can be against me?
Receiving Christ's approval,
He called me Beulah
Before the foundations
Of the earth.
So that marriage wouldn't
Define a woman's worth.
He called me
So I'm **all** woman.
I'm **all** worthy,
Even if I never birth
Children on this earth.
2 John 1:1
I am a chosen lady
Whether I do

Or don't have babies.

I nurture

The calling He gave me.

Whether a house full

Or just me,

I can do all things

Through Christ

Who strengthens me.

It Just *Is*...

How much energy does a flower
Conserve for just being purple?
It just is.
And it flows,
And it knows
It's purple today.
And that's quite OK.
Purple.
It just is...

How much energy does the sky
Conserve for just being blue?
It just is.
And it flows,
And it knows
It's blue today.
And that's quite OK.
Blue.
It just is...

How much energy does grass
Conserve for just being green?
It just is.
And it flows,
And it knows
It's green today.
And that's quite OK.
Green.
It just is...

How much energy can I
Conserve when I realize
I am loved?
It just is.
And it flows,
And I know
I am loved today.
And that's quite OK.
Loved.
It just is...

How much energy can I

Conserve when I realize
I am beautiful?
It just is.
And it flows,
And I know
I am beautiful today.
And that's quite OK.
Beautiful.
It just is...

All of God's creation
Was created to
Glorify the Creator.
So why would The Master
Make anything less than
A masterpiece?
Why would He think
Any less of it?
Any less of he?
Any less of she?
Any less of we?
Any less of me?

It just is...

And it flows,

And He knows

It is a masterpiece today.

And that's quite OK.

Masterpiece.

It just is.

About the Author

Tamika Wells is an American author, poet and multi-passionate creative, gifted in prophetic empathy. Her written and spoken word superpower lies in her innate ability to empower women who are powerful in public but face life circumstances that make them feel pitiful in private. While managing several budding entrepreneurial ventures, Tamika is the CEO and Master Certified Life Coach of Elevate Her Coaching Program. In addition, she is an Emotional Freedom Techniques (EFT) Practitioner; through her firm, Honey Tree Healing, Tamika helps clients heal the love relationship with self and others, breaking recurring cycles of abusive and unhealthy relationship patterns including those of sexual trauma. Her programs are rooted in clients' abilities to experience new transformations, mutually beneficial relationships and even better financial outcomes. Tamika is mother to her adult son and resides in North Carolina with her two kittens, Goodness and Mercy.

Connect with Tamika on Instagram:

@CoachElevateHer & *@SheisTamikaWells*

www.TamikaWells.com

Made in the USA
Middletown, DE
25 August 2022

72282659R00189